THE
TROPICS
AND
ECONOMIC
DEVELOPMENT

A
provocative inquiry
into
the
poverty of nations

Published for
The World Bank

THE
TROPICS
AND
ECONOMIC
DEVELOPMENT

Andrew M. Kamarck
with a foreword by Paul Streeten

The Johns Hopkins University Press
Baltimore and London

The publisher and the World Bank acknowledge with thanks permission from
the copyright holders to reprint extracts from:

Doris Lessing, African Stories. New York: Simon & Schuster, 1965

William and Elizabeth Paddock, We Don't Know How: An Independent
    Audit of What They Call Success in Foreign Assistance. Ames:
    Iowa State University Press, 1973

Library of Congress Cataloging in Publication Data

Kamarck, Andrew M
    The tropics and economic development.
    Bibliography: p.   Includes index.
    1. Tropics—Economic conditions.   2.   Underdeveloped
areas.   I.   International Bank for Reconstruction and
Development.   II.   Title.
HC695.K25   338.1'09172'4   76–17242
ISBN 0–8018–1891–5
ISBN 0–8018–1903–2 paperback

Contents

030495

Maps

Foreword

Comparative figures show that national income per head in tropical and arid subtropical countries is substantially lower than in countries of the Temperate Zone. But most practicing economists who have had occasion to work with "practical" men of affairs have found that these comparisons are met with an objection. When working in the Ministry of Overseas Development, I came across this objection repeatedly, even though some of those who voiced it had earned good degrees in economics! The objection runs: "Your figures don't show that the people in hot climates are that much worse off. For, if you live in the Tropics, you don't need fuel to keep you warm, nor clothes, because there is the sun, nor need you grow so much food because you pick bananas from the trees and the nuts from the bushes."

This myth of the lotus-eating existence of those who dwell in hot climates is crystallized in the well-known story of the Puritan visitor from an advanced industrial country who addresses a man sprawling on the beach: "Why don't you work instead of idling the time away?" "Why should I?" replies the native. "Because you then would earn money." "What would I do with the money?" After enumerating all the wonderful things which, however, do not seem to appeal to the native, the visitor plays his trump card: "If you worked and saved hard enough, you could afford to take a holiday and enjoy yourself in the sun on the beach"; to which the puzzled native replies, "But that's what I am doing now!"

Andrew Kamarck effectively destroys the illusion that the tropical South provides an easier life than the temperate North. On the contrary: development efforts have to be substantially greater to achieve results similar to those realized in the North. More capital is needed for irrigation, more expenditure must be made on the eradication and prevention of diseases, more resources have to be devoted to research and development of appropriate technologies and on mineral exploration.

A hot and humid climate reduces the efficiency of man, cattle, and land. Work generates body heat and is clearly more difficult in a hot climate. Manual laborers wield their tools with a feebler stroke and take more frequent and longer rest pauses than workers in cooler climates, who are normally also healthier and better nourished. Malaria, schistosomiasis, trypanosomiasis, leprosy, onchocerciasis, sleeping sickness, and leishmaniasis—all debilitating or killing tropical diseases—affect one third of the world's population and present major obstacles to development. The recrudescence of malaria in the Gezira region has set back a most promising model of an agricultural cooperative. Schistosomiasis has appeared in irrigated areas with stagnant water. River blindness and sleeping sickness have led to the abandonment of fertile land in Africa. Estimated expenditure on tropical disease research is $30 million a year, which is a tiny fraction of what rich countries spend on research on a single disease alone.

Land erosion of the top soil, through wind and rain, is much more serious in tropical countries. So is leaching (water washing essential soil ingredients downwards), which is particularly serious in tropical areas with high rainfall and is one cause of rapid loss of fertility. Possibly the most important single obstacle to human betterment is the inadequate rainfall in arid tropical zones. (Europeans got a foretaste of what this means in the long drought during the summer of 1976 and their attitude toward clouds began to resemble that of the Indian as Khushwant Singh describes it on page 13.) As a result of high rates of evaporation, irrigation aimed at overcoming water scarcity can lead to salination unless extra care and additional investment are provided for meticulous control of water applications, or unless drainage is installed to carry away surplus water.

The belief may still be prevalent that nothing can be done about the weather—though this belief is not entirely correct and, in any case, better forecasting would help to prepare against, for example, hurricanes and floods. But a good deal can be done, and has not been done, to find solutions to the difficulties presented by the climate. Soils can be enriched and erosion reduced; cattle and people can be better fed and better housed; diseases can be eradicated; refrigeration and air conditioning can be used more widely; buildings and equipment can be better adapted to withstand heat and humidity; insects can be controlled—the list goes on. But all this costs money and requires knowledge and skills. The existing wide gaps in our knowledge of the impact of climate on a whole variety of factors can be reduced. What is needed is cooperative research by geographers, meteorologists, biologists, zoologists, doctors, engineers, agronomists, foresters, and economists whose joint skills should be applied to the solution of these urgent problems. Andrew Kamarck's is a challenging and provocative inquiry into these long neglected problems of development.

But Andrew Kamarck, being a good empiricist, is not interested in the more speculative question: Why has the role of climate in development been so neglected not only in academic literature but also in development plans? This question belongs to the sociology of knowledge, or rather of ignorance and false beliefs. In the days before independence, before the universal right to and the universal possibility of economic growth had become widely proclaimed and when poverty was accepted as the fate of the majority of mankind, climate, together with ethnic and cultural factors, was used as part of the explanation for backwardness. Climate was an ingredient in the doctrine of pessimistic geographical determinism, together with the racial inferiority of the colonial peoples. With independence in the period following World War II, pessimism was replaced by optimism, encouraged by the success of the Marshall Plan. The protest movement of the newly independent elite and the sympathetic or diplomatic responses to this protest of Western intellectuals, politicians, and officials called for the ready transferability of knowledge and skills from advanced to "underdeveloped" (no longer "backward") or, later, "developing" countries. The neglect of the role of climate fitted well into the new optimism. It is part of the stages-of-growth mythology that all countries tread inexorably the same path to eventual "take-off" and self-sustained economic growth; that the speed of this march is determined by savings ratios, investment ratios, and capital-output ratios; and that the role of rich countries is to supply missing components, like foreign exchange or skills. Gunnar Myrdal has called such neglect and ignorance "opportunistic." Not only what we think we know, but also what we don't know, what we neglect, and what we forget, has roots in the social system from which our doctrines grow.

It is important to note that Andrew Kamarck's is not just another unicausal explanation, succeeding those who thought that land, or labor, or capital, or education, or technology were the key to development. Andrew Kamarck makes it quite clear that a major difficulty lies in the fact that the effects of climate can rarely be isolated from the effects of nutrition, health, education and, to some extent, social organization and numerous other conditions. There are relations among all the variables in the social system. The focus on climate is necessary only because it has been neglected.

Is then the growing awareness of the importance of climate and of the environment more generally a sign that we are swinging back to pessimism? Is it an excuse for disengagement from international cooperation, from capital aid and technical assistance? Although disenchantment and pessimism have replaced the easy optimism of the 1950s and early 1960s, this is certainly not the argument of this book. On the contrary: after periods of biased optimism and biased pessimism, each attempting to justify unjustifiable international action or inaction, the former attempting to justify the easy transfer of Western technologies in the expectation of quick results, the latter attempting to justify a retreat from aid and technical assistance, Andrew Kamarck's conclusion is a call to realism. International cooperation to remove real constraints, particularly cooperation in research devoted to solving real problems and cooperation in the consequential investment, would set free the vast human and social potential of billions of people now locked into a hostile environment.

PAUL STREETEN
Warden of
Queen Elizabeth House, Oxford

Oxford
July 1976

Preface

The subject of the Tropics and its relation to economic development is not one on which I began willingly. I felt myself obliged to study this subject because during my work at the World Bank it became more and more evident to me that development economics largely ignores one central fact: most of the obstacles faced by today's developing countries are very different from those that were faced by today's industrialized countries when they were poor.

In addition, I was dissatisfied with the two most prevalent theories that attempt to explain why today's developing countries have lagged in the worldwide process of modern economic growth that started in England more than 200 years ago. The first of these theories—usually unvoiced and often not even consciously recognized by those who believe and act on it—is that the lag of the less developed countries is a consequence of something inferior in the character, ability, or personality of the peoples of the Third World, an inferiority that brings about their low productivity. The second theory, equally unsatisfactory, is that the lag is the result of the industrialized countries' having derived their wealth from exploitation of the peoples of the Third World rather than from their high productivity.

Both theories fly in the face of the facts. Both result in a neglect of the real problems faced by the countries of the Third World and in a diversion of energies into confrontation rather than into the cooperation between the industrialized and the developing countries that is needed if the latter are to develop as rapidly as they are able.

This book fits into a series of other papers that I have worked on in recent years. The series was inspired by reflections on the differences between what seemed evident to me from my quarter of a century's experience in working on problems of the developing countries and what much of standard economic development theory teaches. Other papers in the series include "The Appraisal of Country Economic Performance" (*Economic Development and Cultural Change*, January 1970), " 'Capital' and 'Investment' in Developing

Countries" (*Proceedings of the Truman International Conference on Technical Assistance and Development*, Jerusalem, 1971, and *Finance & Development*, June 1971), and "The Allocation of Aid by Multilateral Institutions" (*Finance & Development*, September 1972).

Most of the initial writing on this book was done while I was on a sabbatical from the World Bank at the Harvard University Center for International Affairs. This was a rewarding experience for me and I am particularly grateful for the hospitality of the Harvard Development Advisory Service and its director, Lester Gordon, for my stay there. During the course of the various revisions of the book, I received valuable criticisms, suggestions, and comments from many people. Among those who were most helpful are: Walter P. Falcon, Stanford Food Research Institute; Carl Gotch, Harvard Development Advisory Service; Dr. Dieter Koch-Weser, Harvard Medical School; H. E. Landsberg, World Meteorological Organization; Donald V. McGranahan, UN Research Institute for Social Development; Edwin M. Martin, Consultative Group on Food Production and Investment; E. S. Mason, Harvard University; Dr. Myron G. Schultz, Center for Disease Control; Joseph J. Stern, Harvard Development Advisory Service; Don Stoops, World Bank Agriculture and Rural Development Department; Charles Weiss, Jr., World Bank Projects Advisory Staff; and the members and readers of the World Bank's editorial committee. I also appreciate the efforts of Brian J. Svikhart, who made a substantial contribution in editing the book and also prepared the index.

ANDREW M. KAMARCK
Director
Economic Development Institute

World Bank
Washington, D.C.
June 1976

THE
TROPICS
AND
ECONOMIC
DEVELOPMENT

1. Introduction

The human being is inseparable from its environment.

ALFRED NORTH WHITEHEAD

Human nature exists and operates in an environment.
And it is not "in" that environment as coins are in a
box, but as a plant in the sunlight and soil.

JOHN DEWEY

Mankind are influenced by various causes, by the climate,
by the religion, by the laws, by the maxims of government, by precedents, morals, and customs; from whence
is formed a general spirit of nations.

MONTESQUIEU

Since the Industrial Revolution began in England around
the middle of the eighteenth century, a continually increasing number of countries have been caught up in the process called economic
development. Development involves many different sets of forces,
and no simple model can explain how and why the process operates
—or fails to operate—in different countries. Recognizing that fact,
this book advances the hypothesis that one of the most important
sets of reasons why a large number of countries have lagged in this
process arises from their location in the Tropics. Broadly stated, the
argument is that:

Compared to the Temperate Zones, there are certain effects of
the tropical climate that, up to the present,
• hinder agriculture;
• handicap mineral exploration; and
• make the population less vigorous through disease and, possibly, through the direct physiological impact of temperature
and humidity.
The effects of tropical climate are not absolute obstacles to economic development, but they do make many of the problems of
economic development in the Tropics sufficiently different from

those in the Temperate Zone countries so that an additional hurdle has to be overcome and, consequently, all other relevant factors being equal, the pace of development in tropical countries tends to be slower.

The popular contrast drawn between the so-called North (or the rich countries) and the South (or poor countries) in the world is wrong: the proper contrast is between the rich Temperate Zones and the poor Tropics. At the beginning of the Second Development Decade, January 1, 1971, most of the countries in the North and South Temperate Zones of the world on the one hand had succeeded in becoming either "rich" countries, with a per capita gross national product (GNP) of more than $1,000, or "middle-income" countries, with a $375 to $1,000 per capita GNP.[1] On the other hand, most of the countries with a tropical climate were "poor"—GNP per capita $100 to $375—or "very poor"—GNP per capita under $100. As John Kenneth Galbraith wrote twenty years earlier: "[If] one marks off a belt a couple of thousand miles in width encircling the earth at the equator one finds within it *no* developed countries . . . Everywhere the standard of living is low and the span of human life is short."[2] The map on pages 6–7 illustrates this statement.

Most recent economic writing on development has paid little or no attention to any possible influence of climate. Purely mathematical growth models make no provision for climatic parameters or variables. There is no mention of climate in the combined list of "characteristics of backward economies" devised by Harvey Leibenstein from various leading economic writers whom he surveyed for this purpose.[3] In Gerald M. Meier's selection of readings that focus "on those problem areas and issues of policy-making that are likely to

1. All dollar figures throughout the text are expressed in current U.S. dollars.
2. "Conditions for Economic Change in Underdeveloped Countries," *Journal of Farm Economics* 33 (November 1951), p. 693. See also United Nations, Department of Economic and Social Affairs, *Report on the World Social Situation with Special Reference to the Problem of Balanced Social and Economic Development* (E/CN.5/512/rev.1/ST/ESA/24), 1961, p. 30: "If the industrialized countries are marked on a map, they will be seen to be located as a rule in a colder climate than the under-developed countries. This correlation with climate is as good as most correlations between non-economic factors and economic development. . . . After receiving perhaps an exaggerated importance in the early part of this century from a number of theorists and then being neglected, the role of climate . . . needs some renewed attention."
3. *Economic Backwardness and Economic Growth: Studies in the Theory of Economic Development* (New York: Wiley, 1957), pp. 39–41.

remain of central concern in future efforts to accelerate development," there is nothing on problems arising out of climate.[4] Albert O. Hirschman, in summarizing theories that Latin Americans and others have presented to explain Latin America's lag in economic development, did not mention climate once.[5] Even John Mellor in his treatise, *The Economics of Agricultural Development*—a book about farming, after all!—does not so much as include an index entry for "weather," "climate," or "Tropics." [6]

Celso Furtado, a leading Latin American economist, did comment in 1963 that existing technology was largely developed for temperate climates and for the combination of resources found in them, and that it is not "readily adaptable to the Brazilian tropics and to the country's peculiar assortment of resources. . . . [E]xtensive acreages of soil with good physical characteristics and adequate water lie idle for lack of an agricultural technique appropriate to them. Particularly cruel is the situation in the poverty-ridden Nordeste [northeast], where some six million acres of such soils go uncultivated." [7] But Furtado's more recent *Obstacles to Development in Latin America* failed to follow up on this perception.

Part of the present neglect of climate as a factor in economic development is probably a strong reaction against earlier theories of geographers, particularly that of Ellsworth Huntington, who maintained that the different climates determined different levels of civilization through direct effects on human energies and achievement. In other words, the level of human achievement is directly affected by the degree to which the weather is moderate and variable.

---

4. *Leading Issues in Economic Development: Studies in International Poverty*, 2nd ed. (New York: Oxford University Press, 1970), p. vii.

5. *Latin American Issues: Essays and Comments* (New York: Twentieth Century Fund, 1961), pp. 3–42. There is similarly no discussion of climate as a force affecting development in the International Economic Association's 1957 conference on "Economic Development for Latin America," in its 1960 conference on "Economic Development for Africa South of the Sahara," or in Charles T. Nisbit's collection of readings, *Latin America: Problems in Economic Development* (New York: Free Press, 1969).

6. *The Economics of Agricultural Development* (Ithaca: Cornell University Press, 1966). Mellor does comment in passing, however, that "[t]ropical agriculture appears to have a special vulnerability to damage from diseases and insects" (p. 108). One of the essential features of the tropical climate is that it favors the evolution of a multiplicity of diseases and pests. I discuss this fact in more detail later.

7. "The Development of Brazil," *Scientific American* 209 (September 1963), p. 216.

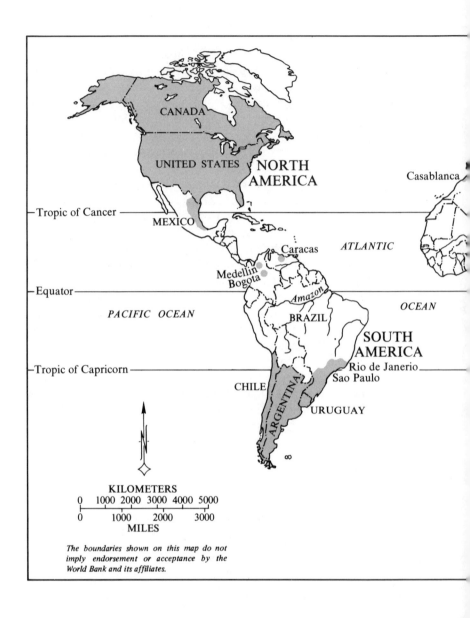

The boundaries shown on this map do not imply endorsement or acceptance by the World Bank and its affiliates.

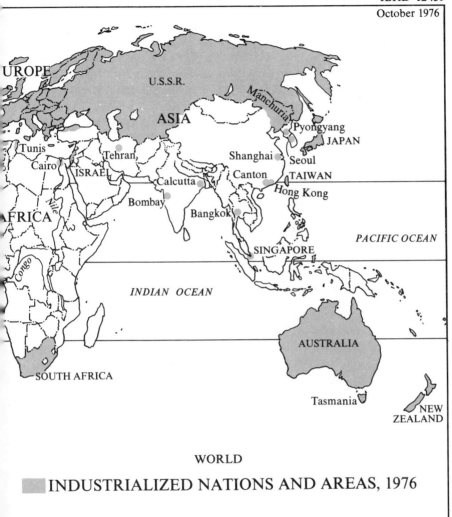

UROPE

U.S.S.R.

ASIA

Manchuria

Pyongyang

JAPAN

Tunis

Tehran

Shanghai

Seoul

Cairo

ISRAEL

Canton

TAIWAN

Calcutta

Hong Kong

Bombay

Bangkok

AFRICA

Nile

Congo

PACIFIC OCEAN

SINGAPORE

INDIAN OCEAN

AUSTRALIA

SOUTH AFRICA

Tasmania

NEW ZEALAND

WORLD

INDUSTRIALIZED NATIONS AND AREAS, 1976

This argument is not very convincing. However, as Charles P. Kindleberger points out: "The arguments against Huntington are telling, but the fact remains that no tropical country in modern times has achieved a high state of economic development. This establishes some sort of presumptive case—for the end result, if not for the means." [8] As I hope to show, Kindleberger has put his finger on the issue: economists were right to be dissatisfied with Huntington's theory, but wrong to assume then that climatic factors should be totally neglected. [9]

W. B. Reddaway has pointed out that the difference between the economics of developed and developing countries lies mainly "in the assumptions which one 'naturally' makes in considering the problem—and all too often fails to specify explicitly. . . . For understanding the economic problems of under-developed countries one needs to develop a new set of instinctive assumptions." [10] Kenneth Boulding also touched on this point: "The principal failure of economics, certainly in the last generation, has been in the field of economic development . . . Development, like economics, has been very much a Temperate Zone product . . . [The] result of imposing Temperate Zone techniques on the tropics, whether in engineering, agriculture or in economics, may easily be disastrous." [11]

In the rich countries where most of the writing on economic problems is done and where those standards are set which economists in developing countries tend to follow, most economic activity is now either independent of climate or increasingly insulated against it. [12] The concentration by economic theorists in rich countries on building highly abstract models has often resulted in analysis that has little relation to any developed economy now or ever likely to be extant. In these rarefied circumstances, it is even less academically rewarding to analyze the real problems that present-day poor countries

8. *Economic Development*, 2nd ed. (New York: McGraw-Hill, 1965), p. 78.

9. In the course of a discussion in December 1971, Albert O. Hirschman commented that part of the reason for the neglect of the effects of climate by development economists in recent years was due to the belief that nothing could be done about them.

10. "The Economics of Under-developed Countries," *Economic Journal* 73 (March 1963), pp. 1–2.

11. "Is Economics Culture-Bound?" *American Economic Review* 60 (May 1970), p. 409.

12. In economic history prior to the Industrial Revolution, it was much more evident that climate was an important factor. See the revealing title by Emmanuel Le Roy Ladurie, *Times of Feast, Times of Famine: A History of Climate Since the Year* 1000, trans. Barbara Bray (London: Allen and Unwin, 1972).

face, which differ from those that are of interest to the rich and middle-income countries. Some problems in poor countries are in fact
such that it is either extremely difficult or impossible to address them
in a mathematical model.

There are a few exceptions to the economists' general disregard of
the development consequences of climate. In discussing some of the
characteristics of poor countries, Paul Streeten says:

> Perhaps the most striking fact is that most underdeveloped
> countries lie . . . between the Tropic of Cancer and Tropic of
> Capricorn. Recent writers have too easily glossed over this fact
> and considered it largely fortuitous. This reveals . . . the re-
> luctance to admit the vast differences in initial conditions with
> which today's poor countries are faced compared with the pre-
> industrial phase of more advanced countries.[13]

13. "How Poor Are the Poor Countries," in *Development in a Divided
World*, ed. Dudley Seers and Leonard Joy (Harmondsworth, Eng.: Penguin,
1971), p. 78. Others among the most perceptive have been Pèter Tamàs Bauer,
Dissent on Development: Studies and Debates in Developing Economics (Cambridge, Mass.: Harvard University Press, 1972), pp. 82, 299; Stephen Enke,
"Economists and Development: Rediscovering Old Truths," *Journal of Eco-
nomic Literature* 7 (December 1969), pp. 1127, 1131; S. Herbert Frankel,
"Economic Changes in Africa in Historical Perspective," in *Economic Develop-
ment in the Long Run*, ed. Alexander J. Youngston (London: Allen and Unwin,
1972), pp. 214–15; Benjamin H. Higgins, *Economic Development: Principles,
Problems, and Policies*, rev. ed. (New York: Norton, 1968), pp. 209–33; William
O. Jones, "Environment, Technical Knowledge, and Economic Development in
Tropical Africa," *Food Research Institute Studies* 5 (1965), pp. 101–16; L. Don
Lambert, "The Role of Climate in the Economic Development of Nations,"
Land Economics 47 (November 1971), pp. 339–44; and Gunnar Myrdal, *Asian
Drama: An Inquiry into the Poverty of Nations* (New York: Twentieth Century
Fund, 1968), Appendix 10. See also Andrew M. Kamarck, *The Economics of
African Development*, rev. ed. (New York: Praeger, 1971), chs. I and V.
Abdoulaye Wade in his study of the west African economy emphasized the
close relation between climate, on the one hand, and agriculture, the system of
property rights, and the economy on the other; see *Economie de l'Ouest Africain
(Zone Franc): Unité et Crossance* (Paris: Présence Africaine, 1964), pp. 28–31.
W. Arthur Lewis observed that "[t]he most important natural resources are climate, fresh water, fertile soil, useful minerals, and a topography which facilitates
transportation"; see *The Theory of Economic Growth* (Homewood, Ill.: Irwin,
1955), p. 51. Lewis continued: "It is clear that extremes of temperature are
unfavorable. Nevertheless, civilizations have flourished in the past in countries
varying very widely in their climates, from the hot river valleys of the sub-tropics
to the high altitudes of Mexico and Peru . . . [T]he association between growth
and temperate climates is a very recent phenomenon in human history" (p. 53).
In the sweep of human history over the millenia, it is quite possible that, two or
three hundred years from now, there will be little difference in the material eco-

There are a number of reasons why we need a more accurate diagnosis of the real problems of development. The first is fairly obvious: if we do not know what the obstacles are, we cannot pursue the proper policies to eliminate or to avoid them. (In fact, better understanding of the obstacles created by the tropical climate is now leading to new policies designed by the international development community to overcome or to avoid these obstacles.) The second reason for better understanding is to avoid the disillusionment and despair already setting in among many people over the prospects for development in the less developed countries. This is the second phase of the optimistic bias to which Streeten referred. Without an appreciation for the magnitude of these difficulties, people soon suffer disappointment over the rate of progress in overcoming them. Finally, a proper understanding of the different and greater obstacles faced by the developing countries in the Tropics will help keep people in the richer countries from falling into the arrogant or racist conclusion that the reason developing countries are poor is that their peoples are somehow inherently inferior.[14]

---

nomic levels of tropical and temperate countries. But at present it is important to identify the reasons why tropical countries have lagged during the last two hundred years in the process of modern economic growth.

14. This last point is illustrated well by William and Elizabeth Paddock in *We Don't Know How: An Independent Audit of What They Call Success in Foreign Assistance* (Ames: Iowa State University Press, 1973), pp. 170–71:

> I spent an evening some years ago in the home of Francisco Brennand, a well-known Brazilian artist. . . . Brennand said his ancestors are Irish [which] caused one of the guests to comment that it was too bad the tropics had not had the benefit of immigration from northern Europe. . . . "Your Irish Recife would be quite a different place than it is today."
>
> "I doubt it," Brennand's wife interjected. "My ancestors were Dutch, and they came here 400 years ago. In fact, this whole area was settled by the Dutch." . . . It is wrong to blame the poverty of the tropics on the people who settled them—the Dutch are certainly not lazy, nor are the Portuguese who came later; after all, it was the Portuguese who opened up the Great Age of Discovery. No, there is little difference among the world's peoples in this respect.

A similar point is made more bluntly by the noted geographer Charles A. Fisher in *South-east Asia: A Social, Economic, and Political Geography*, 2nd ed. (New York: Dutton, 1966), p. 61:

> In the writer's experience a three-year sojourn in the jungles of Thailand went far to counter the optimistic possibilism which appeared so eminently reasonable in the air-conditioned clubs of Singapore. And if the possibilists seriously maintain that the rigours of the humid tropical environment are a wholly inadequate explanation of the retarded development of these regions, does their philosophy really amount to anything

————•••————

This book first attempts to outline major characteristics of the tropical climates that are significant to economic development. Next it considers the adverse effects of tropical climate on agriculture—the quality of soil, the quantity and frequency of rainfall, and the multiplicity of pests and disease—and explores the first systematic international effort, now under way, to mobilize the knowledge necessary to cope with these effects. The next section briefly indicates how the tropical climate adversely influences exploration for mineral resources. The final section outlines the widespread extent and impact of diseases in the Tropics that directly affect man's economic activity.[15]

None of this is to claim that climate has a mechanical one-to-one relation to economic development, nor that climate with its effects is the only ruling constraint on economic development, nor that if the effects of climate were removed as a constraint in today's poor countries development would be unbounded. Rather, in today's poor countries climatic factors have hampered economic development through their impact on agriculture—directly or through the diseases and pests afflicting animals and plants—on mineral discovery, and on man himself through disease. These effects need to be better understood. High priority should be given investment for research to find ways to minimize the adverse impacts of climate and to turn the particular manifestations of local climate to advantage. As economic development proceeds in a country, it will become easier to eliminate or to avoid the worst effects of tropical climate, and climate will become less important as a factor in development.

other than a reformulation, however unintentional, of the old doctrine of white supremacy?

15. There may be still other ways in which the tropical climate has an impact on economic development that more research may be able to expose. Ambassador Edwin M. Martin has commented in a letter to me that in some parts of the Tropics the absence of alternating productive and unproductive seasons may adversely affect basic attitudes toward savings and investment. (Maeterlinck's classic study of the bee observed that bees stop storing honey when taken to areas where a continuous supply of food is available the year round.) Also, based on his experience in the Tropics, Joseph J. Stern commented in a personal communication that the impact of some tropical climates is often such that it raises physical capital costs. For example, it is difficult to use wood in construction without thorough and costly protection against termites, and the wear and tear on machinery is greater under tropical conditions than in temperate climates. A similar point was made by the French Under Secretary for Overseas Departments and Territories: "The reason for Guiana's underdevelopment is simple. Equipment expenses there are four times higher than at home because of the climate." See Oliver Stirn quoted in _Newsweek_ 86 (October 27, 1975), international ed., p. 14.

At the same time, just because a country is becoming richer, the adverse effects of climate become less economically important. As individual incomes rise, according to Engel's law, a smaller and smaller proportion of income is spent on food. The proportion of GNP produced in agriculture will therefore tend to drop and, consequently, climatic factors affecting agriculture will become less important to national economic development. The relative importance in the development process of possessing mineral resources varies inversely with the level of development. As GNP rises, the possession of natural resources becomes progressively less important. Finally, growth in GNP enables greater expenditure on health problems, attenuating this impact of climate.[16]

16. Today, the climatic obstacles to economic development of the poor countries remain mostly in the Tropics. Thirty years ago they were probably also important in the sub-Tropics. A large part of the initiation of rapid economic growth in Mediterranean Europe after World War II is undoubtedly due to the economic activity in western and northwestern Europe, but an important factor may also have been the eradication of some important diseases after the war.

Item: Before World War II, Greece was an intense focus of malaria; in some years reported, cases totaled around a quarter of the entire population. Malaria was eradicated in the later 1940s. Would Greece's recent rapid economic growth have been possible otherwise? [See Jacques M. May, *Studies in Disease Ecology* (New York: Hafner, 1961), p. 200.]

Item: "Until malaria was wiped out [in Corsica], no one farmed [on the eastern plain]. Today this plain accounts for 60 percent of Corsica's agricultural production." [Paul-Andre Carlotti, chief of service for the Société pour la mise-en-valeur agricole de la Corse, quoted in Robert Cairns, "Sunny Corsica, French Morsel in the Mediterranean," *National Geographic* 144 (September 1973), p. 420.]

Item: In the United States up to World War II, the southern states were clearly far poorer than the northern. In 1938 the South was called by Franklin Roosevelt "the nation's economic problem No. 1." In the 1880s—when the first data are available—the ratio between per capital personal incomes in the three poorest states (that is, with per capital personal incomes well under $100) and the three highest income states in the North or West was 1 to 6.5. Malaria and hookworm were not eradicated until after World War II—indeed, over a million cases a year were still reported in the 1920s. Is it solely a coincidence that since then the South has been one of the fastest growing sections of the United States and that by 1966 the personal income ratio had narrowed to about 1 to 1.9? [See Mahinder D. Chaudhry, "Economic Distance among Regions: A Statistical Analysis," *Economic Development and Cultural Change* 19 (July 1971), pp. 527–28.]

We can see this process at work today in Nepal. The southern plains, or Terai, were virtually unpopulated until the early 1950s because of malaria. Since then malaria has been eradicated and hill people have begun to move to the Terai leaving their poorer eroded farms in the hills.

2. The Tropics

The farmer who has lived through drought will never
forget it. Years afterwards, away from Africa, in the wet
climate of a northern country, he will start up at night,
at the sound of a sudden shower of rain, and cry, "At
last, at last."

KAREN BLIXEN, *Out of Africa*

An Indian's attitude towards clouds and rain remains
fundamentally different from that of the Westerner. To
the one, clouds symbolize hope; to the other, they suggest
despair. The Indian scans the heavens and if cumulus
clouds blot out the sun his heart fills with joy. The Westerner looks up and if there is no silver lining edging the
clouds his depression deepens.

KHUSHWANT SINGH

A tropical climate affects all of Africa except South Africa
and portions of countries in the extreme north of the continent; all
of South America except Argentina, Chile, and Uruguay; Central
America and the Caribbean including southern Mexico; and south
and southeast Asia. There are three principal types of tropical climates, as the map on page 14 illustrates: wet equatorial, dry tropical,
and alternately wet and dry tropical (monsoon). The wet equatorial,
or humid, tropical climates lie mainly within 5° of the equator. In
these latitudes some rain falls in all months, and usually totals 200
to 300 centimeters a year (roughly 75 to 120 inches). The wet equatorial climate is characterized by constant heat, rainfall, and humidity. In South America these climates occur in the Amazon Basin
of Brazil, Surinam, French Guiana, Guyana, and Venezuela; in
Africa, in the Congo (Zaïre) Basin and in a strip along most of the
northern coast of the Gulf of Guinea in west Africa, and in east
Africa along the coast of Kenya and Tanzania and the east coast of
Madagascar; and over parts of Malaya, Indonesia, Papua New
Guinea, and many of the Pacific islands.

IBRD 12440
October 1976

U.S.S.R.

MONGOLIA

N. KOREA

JAPAN

TURKEY

AFGHANISTAN

CHINA

LEB.
ISRAEL
JORDAN

IRAN

BHUTAN

S. KOREA

IRAQ
KUWAIT
QATAR
SAUDI
ARABIA

PAKISTAN

NEPAL

INDIA

LAO P.D.R.

TAIWAN

Tropic of Cancer

UN.
ARAB
EM.
OMAN

BANGLA-
DESH

HONG KONG

YEMEN
ARAB REP.

P.D.R.
OF YEMEN

BURMA
THAILAND

VIET-
NAM

PHILIPPINES

ASIA AND THE
WESTERN PACIFIC

SRI
LANKA

KHMER
REP.

MALAYSIA

SINGAPORE

Equator

INDONESIA

PAPUA
NEW GUINEA

TROPICAL CLIMATES

Dry

Wet

Alternately wet and dry

Subtropical highlands

Highlands over 5,000 feet

AUSTRALIA

Tropic of
Capricorn

THE AMERICAS

Kilometers
0   1000 2000 3000
0   1000   2000
Miles

CUBA

Tropic of Cancer

HAITI
DOMINICAN REP.

MEXICO

BELIZE

JAMAICA

BARBADOS

GUATEMALA
EL SALVADOR
HONDURAS
COSTA RICA
PANAMA
Canal Zone

NICARAGUA

TRINIDAD & TOBAGO
GUYANA
SURINAM
FR. GUIANA

VENEZUELA

COLOMBIA

AFRICA

ECUADOR

Equator

TUNISIA

MOROCCO

FORMER
SP. SAHARA

ALGERIA

ARAB REP.
OF LIBYA

ARAB REP.
OF EGYPT

Tropic
of Cancer

PERU

BRAZIL

MAURITANIA

MALI

NIGER

CHAD

SUDAN

BOLIVIA

SENEGAL
THE
GAMBIA
GUINEA
BISSAU
GUINEA
SIERRA
LEONE

UPPER
VOLTA

F.T.A.I.

PARAGUAY

Tropic
of
Capricorn

CHILE

CEN.
AFR. REP.

ETHIOPIA

SOMALIA

URUGUAY

LIBERIA
IVORY COAST
GHANA
TOGO
BENIN
CAMEROON
EQ. GUINEA
GABON
CONGO

RWANDA
BURUNDI

UGANDA

KENYA

ZAIRE

Equator

TANZANIA

ANGOLA

MALAWI
MOZAMBIQUE

ARGENTINA

ZAMBIA

RHODESIA
BOTSWANA

MADA-
GASCAR

NAMIBIA

Tr. of
Capricorn

SOUTH AFRICA

SWAZILAND
LESOTHO

The boundaries shown on this map do not
imply endorsement or acceptance by the
World Bank and its affiliates.

The dry tropical climates tend to be centered on the Tropics of Cancer and Capricorn and range between the latitudes 15° and 30° north and south. The climate is dominated by dry air masses descending and moving away from the subtropical high pressure cells over the large land masses. Hot, arid climates and desert areas result, where rainfed agriculture is practically impossible. These climates embrace north Africa, Arabia, Iran, northwestern India, Australia, and part of the Pacific coast of South America.

Regions lying between the wet equatorial climate and the belts of dry tropical climate have alternately wet and dry tropical climates. These regions tend to have a wet season when the sun is overhead and a dry season when the sun is lower. These alternating wet and dry climates cover the areas lying roughly between 5° and 15° north and south in South America; west and central Africa, and Australia, and as far north as 25° in parts of southeast Asia. A similar climate largely covers east Africa in equatorial and higher latitudes.

> Within [this area] . . . there is in fact a continuously variable succession of climates blending into each other. At one extreme is a climate with high total precipitation falling in a two-peak rainy season occupying most of the year, with only short intervening drier spells of reduced rainfall. . . . At the other extreme is a climate with low total rainfall in one short wet season, and a long dry season." [1]

Rainfall and Heat

Although the tropical climate actually comprises several types of environmental conditions, a few generalizations have economic implications that are valid in most cases. Tropical climate is not *temperate* in its essential sense of moderation. Rainfall rather than temperature determines the seasons, the variation of rainfall from year to year and within the year is considerable and unpredictable, and the average temperature in the coldest month is at least 18°C (64°F).

Rainfall in the Tropics is usually too much or too little. *Average annual rainfall* means little when one year may receive three times as much rain as the next, or when it does not rain evenly throughout a

---

1. Cyril C. Webster and Peter N. Wilson, *Agriculture in the Tropics* (London: Longman, 1966), pp. 5–6.

given season of the year but falls in torrents within brief periods. The extremes are often almost absurd: in July 1972, 4.4 meters (14.5 feet) of rain fell on Luzon, on which much of the economic effort of the Philippines has been concentrated. The rice crop on 1 million acres was destroyed. Also lost was 30 percent of the sugar crop, which dominates Philippine export earnings. Even yearly variations over so large a river basin such as the Volta, which drains over 103,500 square kilometers in western Africa (about 40,000 square miles or an area comparable in size to Great Britain), are very great. At Akosombo, near the Volta's mouth, the flow averages 3,500 to 9,800 cubic meters (125,000 to 350,000 cubic feet) a second at the peak and only about 28 cubic meters (1,000 cubic feet) at the low. Drought tends to come in the hottest and windiest part of the year, so that loss of water by evaporation and transpiration is high. "The ideal conditions, in which the right amount of water is available in the right place at the right time, are only rarely achieved under natural conditions in the . . . tropics." [2]

Rain is a preoccupation for most people throughout the Tropics. A remark by *Washington Post* reporter Jim Hoagland on Africa applies to most of the Tropics: "More than 85 percent of Africa's 300 million people eke out their livings as peasant farmers, and a failure of the rains to come can be a devastating economic disaster. If the question, 'How do Africans live?' means how do most of them spend the majority of their time, the answer probably is 'Thinking about rain.' Life tends to be organized around it, in the way that consumer goods are the centerpiece of Western societies." [3] In 1973 the world became aware of the tragic drought in the six west African countries bordering the Sahara—Chad, Mali, Mauritania, Nigeria, Senegal, and Upper Volta—following a decade of low and badly distributed rainfall and three years of severe drought. Fragmentary in-

2. Bramwell W. Hodder, *Economic Development in the Tropics* (London: Methuen, 1968), p. 25. A World Bank expert on raising livestock in the Latin American Tropics has noted that "the risks involved in livestock farming operations in Latin America are not appreciated fully, particularly by people from the European environment where climatic predictability is high and markets are generally secure. In most Latin American countries, ranching is carried out in the areas where the most predictable thing about the climate is its unpredictability and no one can forecast the next drought or flood." Robert Milford, "World Bank Lending for Livestock Development in Latin America," restricted circulation memorandum of the Agriculture Projects Department, World Bank (October 1971), p. 7.

3. "Africa: Fragments in the Mind," *Washington Post* (February 18, 1973), p. B1.

formation indicated half of Senegal's groundnut crop was lost, 30 to 40 percent of the cattle in the region died, and around one-third of the 30 million population was affected by severe malnutrition and hunger.

Continuous heat and the absence of frost mean that life and reproduction go on throughout the year. The great executioner of nature, winter, is absent. No winter temperatures constrain continuous plant growth or the continuous reproduction and growth of all other kinds of life: weeds, insects, birds, parasitic fungi, spider mites, eelworms, microbes and all kinds of viruses, pests, and parasites on man, his animals, and his crops. Life over most of the Tropics therefore takes on an infinite multiplicity of forms, but fierce competition results and only a relatively few individuals in every generation of any species survive in any one place. The conditions are ideal for rapid evolutionary change to adapt to any new opportunities.[4] (It is not at all surprising that evidence now indicates that even man first evolved in Africa.[5])

Economic Implications

These central biological parameters of the Tropics have considerable economic implications. Because of the multiplicity of species and the rapid evolutionary potential of the Tropics, there is a high probability that any new plant or animal introduced into an area by man will soon be attacked by some rapidly multiplying enemy. A crop successfully established always runs the considerable risk of attracting some new pest that has suddenly appeared. For example: "coffee rust which eliminated the arabica coffee industry in Ceylon [Sri Lanka]; . . . blister blight of tea before control measures were found in Ceylon, South India and Indonesia; 'sudden death' in the Zanzibar cloves; 'swollen shoot' in West Africa cocoa;

4. Douglas H. K. Lee, *Climate and Economic Development in the Tropics* (New York: Harper, 1957), pp. 32–36.
5. The multiplicity of species shows itself in every field. Preston E. James and Hibberd V. B. Kline note: "In one square mile of the Island of Trinidad where a special study of the forest composition was made, nearly three thousand distinct species of trees and plants were identified." See *A Geography of Man* (Waltham, Mass.: Blaisdell, 1966), p. 72. Lumbering as a result is quite different from lumbering in Temperate Zones. In the Tropics, because there may be only one or two trees of a particular genus per hectare, the lumberjack is engaged in an activity that is more like hunting than mass production, and costs go up.

'wither-tip' of Dominican limes; and Panama disease of 'Gros Michel' bananas." [6] The Philippines became self-sufficient in rice in 1967 but had to import rice again in 1971 because of a major outbreak of disease among the new rice varieties.[7]

The Tropics are littered with the ruins of development projects that refused to recognize these special problems. A British Colonial Development Corporation million-dollar chicken-raising scheme in The Gambia was completely wrecked by a disease that killed off chickens by the hundreds of thousands. A similar cause wrecked the Overseas Food Corporation's pig-raising scheme in Queensland. The Richard Toll rice-growing scheme in Senegal has not yet learned to cope with the hundreds of thousands of weaverbirds (Quelea) that descend on the paddies each year when the rice is ripe. The Ford Motor Company tried for twenty years, beginning in 1927, to establish rubber plantations in the Amazon Basin of Brazil. Because of health problems that occurred in spite of massive help from the U.S. government during World War II, as well as tree blight and infertile soil, Ford finally gave up, losing practically the whole of its investment of $15 million.[8] The Gezira Scheme in Sudan started with splendid crops but after a few years "the virgin land . . . appeared to be worthless, filthy with weed and foul with disease." [9] Only the fact that the Gezira company recognized the critical importance of research in the Tropics kept the whole scheme from collapsing in disaster. The tropical Northern Territory of Australia can show numerous examples of failures. In the 1950s, a California consortium invested in a rice project at Humpty Doo and produced small crops with large costs. A Texas company invested in a sorghum-growing project at Tipperary Station, which never produced a profitable crop.[10]

6. Gordon Wrigley, Tropical Agriculture: The Development of Production (New York, Praeger, 1969), p. 215.

7. Food and Agriculture Organization of the United Nations, FAO Commodity Review and Outlook, 1971–72 (Rome, 1972), p. 47. Similar problems, but to a much lesser degree, confront agriculture in the Temperate Zones also— in the United States in 1970 a new virus suddenly became a major threat to the corn crop, but after the winter of 1970–71 it as suddenly disappeared.

8. Mark Perlman, "Some Economic Aspects of Public Health Programs in Underdeveloped Areas," in The Economics of Health and Medical Care (Ann Arbor: University of Michigan, 1964), p. 290.

9. Arthur Gaitskell, Gezira: A Story of Development in the Sudan (London: Faber and Faber, 1959), p. 144.

10. Kenneth MacLeish, "The Top End of Down Under," National Geographic 143 (February 1973), p. 163.

The experience of some of the recent settlers in Amazonia was typical and could have been foreseen: "[T]heir first harvest was excellent, but the second was bad and the third catastrophic. [The settlers] returned to the Northeast even poorer than when they left." [11]

Consider two brief examples of some aspects of climate's impact on two areas, Africa and northeast Brazil. It is not possible to understand African economic history without analyzing the ways in which it has been affected by the tropical climate, nor to understand the particular regional pattern of Brazil's economic development without considering the role played by climate.

Africa is preeminently tropical among the continents. Over 75 percent of Africa's 30 million square kilometers are in the Tropics. Only countries hugging the top of the continent and South Africa, Swaziland, and Lesotho on its southern tip escape a predominantly tropical climate. The equator almost exactly bisects the continent; it is about 4,000 kilometers (2,500 miles) from the equator to the northern crown and 3,750 kilometers (2,300 miles) to the southern tip. Climate is a pervasive and continuing influence on Africa's development; added to other difficult geographical features in earlier centuries, it isolated Africa from the rest of the world. Yellow fever and malaria levied a heavy toll of death on all visitors to tropical Africa. Trypanosomiasis carried by the tsetse fly killed horses and cattle and made it impossible to get to the interior from the coast using animal transport.[12] Commerce had to depend on human porters, the most costly and inefficient of all transport systems. Thus, aside from the other grave difficulties of the Tropics, the transport obstacle alone was quite sufficient to postpone for centuries any appreciable economic development in tropical Africa.

Southern Brazil has benefited from the fact that, because of altitude, its tropical climates do not coincide exactly with the Tropics on the globe.[13] The average temperature in the Tropics usually drops by 1°C for every 550 meters of elevation, or about 1°F for every 1,000 feet. The higher altitudes of the interior foster relatively cool climates so that the highlands of southern Brazil are climatically

11. "Brazil Steps Up Effort to Settle Amazonia," *Washington Post* (October 17, 1974), p. A43.
12. See also pages 38–42.
13. Refer to the map on page 14.

similar to the eastern Appalachians of the United States.[14] It is precisely in this more favorable climate that Brazil's economic development has reached a middle-income per capita level. The northeast of Brazil, the country's problem area with a population of around 30 million, is dominated by an ill-defined wedge of tropical dry climate situated between a humid strip along the east coast and the tropical wet-and-dry savanna stretching north and west to the Amazon rain forest. Brazil's northeast is subject to random, recurrent droughts that may continue from one to three years—the most recent one lasted from February 1970 to March 1971. These droughts effectively bring development plans to a halt. Although the droughts are a major obstacle—perhaps the biggest one to economic development—development approaches heretofore have tended to invest mainly in fixed capital of various kinds rather than in necessary research to find out how best to handle the droughts. Over the last fifty years many dams have been built, but little use has been made of the water for irrigation, in part because of what Albert O. Hirschman characterizes as a "lack of knowledge of the terrain and soils." [15] In fact, there may be some doubt whether irrigation makes sense at all. Hirschman noted that because of high evaporation in reservoirs it was necessary to collect all the rain falling on 100 hectares for a year to get enough water to irrigate 1 hectare.

Most of northern Brazil and the countries bordering Brazil in the north and west are within the humid Tropics; these lands remain largely undeveloped and unpopulated. Michael Nelson estimates that only 12 to 15 percent of the total area and 17 to 20 percent of the agricultural potential have been exploited.[16] The authors of a United Nations soil resources report reason that much of the unfarmed land in Latin America lies within the humid Tropics because the inability to understand the dynamic nature of the soil system there results in disaster. The experience in these areas has been one of initial high hopes followed by failure. Survival has often meant following the shifting cultivation system developed by indigenous farmers in rich areas throughout the world. The authors conclude that "it is clear that the greatest increases in agricultural production

14. Preston E. James, *Introduction to Latin America: The Geographic Background of Economic and Political Problems* (New York: Odyssey, 1964), p. 33.

15. Albert O. Hirschman, *Journeys Toward Progress: Studies of Economic Policymaking in Latin America* (New York: Twentieth Century Fund, 1963), p. 51.

16. Michael Nelson, *The Development of Tropical Lands: Policy Issues in Latin America* (Baltimore: Johns Hopkins University Press, 1973), p. 36n.

may be expected from more intensive utilization of the humid temperate zone soils rather than new agricultural endeavour on the soils of the humid tropics; and from more efficient use of the humid temperate zone tropics . . ." [17]

17. A. C. S. Wright and J. Bennema, *The Soil Resources of Latin America*, FAO/Unesco Project on World Soil Resources Report no. 18 (Rome, 1965), pp. 113–15.

3. Soils

The soil comes first. It is the basis, the foundation of farming. Without it, nothing; with poor soil, poor farming, poor living; with good soil, good farming and living. An understanding of good farming begins with an understanding of the soil.

HENRY L. AHLGREN,
1948 U.S. Department of Agriculture Yearbook

A principal characteristic distinguishing tropical countries from rich and middle-income countries is their comparatively greater ignorance of how they might best exploit and improve the soil. In the main, the basic farming conditions related to the character of the soils in tropical countries are so different from those of the Temperate Zone countries that dealing with them requires building another body of knowledge altogether. That is one of the important facts about economic development in today's poor countries. Agriculture is the dominant economic sector in developing countries, yet these countries cannot follow the path trod by today's rich nations when they in turn were poor because the basic agricultural conditions in the less developed countries are different.

The first aim of this chapter is to outline some of the major soil problems dominating tropical agriculture and holding back the economic development of tropical countries. Several points expanded below deserve stress from the outset. First, not all tropical soils are equally problematic. Second, there are special problems in tropical agriculture that are major obstacles to economic growth and need to be specifically recognized as such. Third, these obstacles may not be insuperable; with sufficient research they may be overcome or bypassed.[1]

1. The position is summarized by two world authorities on agriculture. Sir Joseph Hutchinson states:

Good soil is much like a complex living organism. Its skeleton is made up of numerous tiny mineral soil particles aggregated into a firm and flexible structure. Intermingled with this skeleton is the organic substance, the humus, that is the product of bacteria action on plant litter. In less than half a kilogram of fertile soil there may be 500 million fungi, 500 million protozoa, 10 billion bacteria, and 400 billion algae. Aside from their general function of creating humus, these organisms often perform specific and essential functions. For example, the successful establishment of the rapidly growing North American Monterey pine (*Pinus radiata*) in forestry plantations in eastern Africa depended on cultivating not only the seed but also the particular fungus with which the tree roots have a close cooperative relation.

For all these organisms to exist, the soil structure must be such that it can obtain freely circulating air and water. In the Tropics, the soil has to be protected against the heat of the sun, which would burn away the organic matter and kill the microorganisms, and it has to be protected from the direct blows of the torrential rains, which would crush the structure of the soil, seal off the underlying soil from the air, and leach out the minerals or carry them so far into the earth that the plant roots could not reach them. When the soil is laid bare and exposed to the elements, its temperature rises and the sun hastens the oxidation and disappearance of the humus. Wide variation in temperature occurring in the Tropics between day

---

[The] impressive feature of tropical agriculture is the extent to which soils under tropical conditions are still subject to the factors causing deterioration which have been so largely overcome in temperate regions. . . . [We] have not yet achieved an adequate knowledge of the basic principles of fertility in tropical soils to enable us to do more than speculate on how we shall get to the position that we can establish a rising spiral of fertility to match the rising population pressure. There has been enough imaginative soil and agronomic work to show in a few places that this is not beyond our capacity . . .

See Hutchinson's "Comment" in *Agricultural Development and Economic Growth*, ed. Herman M. Southworth and Bruce F. Johnston (Ithaca: Cornell University Press, 1967), p. 231. Charles E. Kellogg adds that he "expects that 'some day' the most productive agriculture of the world will be mostly in the Tropics, especially in the humid parts. . . . Whether 'some day' is 25, 50, 100 or some other number of years, depends on how rapidly institutions for education, research, and the other public and private sectors of agriculture will develop." See *Agricultural Development and Economic Growth*, p. 233.

and night accelerates the mechanical disintegration of the soil. Finally, rains and wind erode the soil.[2]

Generally soils, with the exception of alluvial or recent volcanic soils, are poor over most of the Tropics because they contain little organic material. Tropical vegetation often looks rich and luxuriant, but appearances are deceiving. Even in dense forests, soils are usually thin and have low fertility. In the forests, decaying plants and trees constantly return to the supporting soil the elements they borrowed from it. An equilibrium is maintained—a precarious one, with very small reserves.

One significant impact of some tropical climates on agriculture is the pattern of rainfall confronting farmers. Generally speaking, the one- to three-month period before the rains break is the driest and hottest time of the year. Webster and Wilson note that this makes the peasant farmers' preparation of the dry, hard ground for planting particularly arduous.[3] By comparison, temperate climates experience cold weather precipitation that exceeds evaporation; the soil in those regions therefore becomes charged with a reserve of water for the new growing season. Moist soil is easier to work. In tropical Africa, the pattern of rainfall and the relation between precipitation and rates of evaporation also result in frequent drought or flood. Productive periods must be sandwiched between these droughts and floods. Consequently, proper soil and water management and careful timing of farm operations are vital in Africa. The

---

2. David B. Grigg notes in *The Harsh Lands: A Study in Agricultural Development* (New York: St. Martin's, 1970), pp. 215–16:

[F]rom 0° to 20°C there is an increasing supply of organic matter and humus, above 20°C the surplus diminishes, and at 25°C the rate of decomposition exceeds the rate of formation. . . . Under the cover of primary rain forest the temperature of the surface soil is between 20°C and 25°C, so that humus formation is in equilibrium. . . . The humus content of rain forest soils is low, between 1 and 3 percent in the upper few centimeters but this is constantly maintained by the annual additions of organic matter from the forest cover. . . . The nutrient cycle is sufficient to maintain growth, even if only in precarious equilibrium. . . . If the forest cover is removed, micro-climatic conditions at the soil level are abruptly changed and the closed nutrient cycle is broken . . . the soil loses its protective cover and is exposed to intense rainfall. Soil temperatures are significantly raised when the shade provided by the forest is removed, the humus is decomposed more rapidly than it is formed. Heavy rain destroys the crumb structure of the soil, and fine particles are washed into the soil destroying porosity.

3. Webster and Wilson, *Agriculture in the Tropics*, pp. 6–7.

different water regimes of Africa also require different approaches to such things as the application of fertilizers and different techniques of plant protection.[4]

Laterites and Shifting Cultivation

Over a very large part of the humid Tropics the soil has turned into laterite.[5] Through leaching, the main plant foods or assimilable bases and phosphorus have been removed from the top horizons of the earth. What is left is a reddish mottled clay, consisting almost entirely of oxides of iron and hydroxide of aluminum that tend to solidify upon exposure to air.[6] While laterite makes useful building material—the Angkor Wat in Kampuchea (formerly the Khmer Republic) is built of it—these so-called tropical red and yellow earths that cover the greater part of the humid Tropics are either agriculturally poor or virtually useless. This soil composition accounts for some of the large iron ore deposits in the Tropics, especially in the Philippines and Rhodesia, and explains the large bauxite deposits mined in tropical countries for the aluminum industry. The map on page 26 indicates the extent of laterites throughout the world.

4. Montague Yudelman, "Imperialism and the Transfer of Agricultural Techniques," restricted circulation memorandum of the Agriculture and Rural Development Department, World Bank (Washington D.C., August 1972), p. 6.

5. There has been considerable ambiguity as to the use of the term *laterite*. H. Vine, writing on soils in Webster and Wilson, *Agriculture in the Tropics*, p. 33, cautions that:

> Almost all soil scientists now agree that the word "laterite" should only refer to the forms and varieties of sesquioxidic material that either become hard on exposure or already have hardened, and may or may not be present in "latosols" and can also occur in other soils. Recently the American Soil Survey decided to substitute a new term "plinthite" for "laterite" in this sense . . .

But *plinthite* has not been widely adopted as yet. Some latosols are sometimes also called *ferrallitic soils* and *ferrallites*. Vine continues, p. 34:

> But latosols, according to the most widely held general concept . . . include the majority of the reddish and yellowish-brown soils of the humid and sub-humid tropics. [Among their significant economic characteristics, they are] formed on uplands and slopes by process of decomposition, oxidation and leaching. . . . [T]he low content of minerals such as biotite and lime-sodas felspar is significant because this means a lack of reserves of nutrients.

6. Fisher, *South-east Asia*, p. 51.

ASIA AND THE
WESTERN PACIFIC

LATERITE SOILS
AND RAIN FORESTS
OF THE WORLD

Laterites and latosols

Rain forests

THE AMERICAS

AFRICA

Kilometers
0   1000 2000 3000

0   1000   2000
Miles

Tropic of Cancer

Equator

Tropic of
Capricorn

The boundaries shown on this map do not
imply endorsement or acceptance by the
World Bank and its affiliates.

Over the centuries, the inhabitants of many tropical countries established a method of cultivation to meet the soil conditions confronting them. Farmers in most of sub-Saharan Africa, the Philippines, the highlands and many lowland areas of Indonesia's outer islands, parts of India and Sri Lanka, and the tropical rain forests of Central and South America developed "shifting" or "semi-nomadic" cultivation. Shifting tillage, still by far the most common type of agriculture in use in the humid tropics, cultivates fields for a few years, then allows them to revert to bush jungle to restore their fertility over periods lasting as long as twenty-five years.[7] Shifting cultivation makes survival possible under difficult conditions—but only at a bare existence level. The practice of shifting cultivation has also meant that often one of the main advantages of agricultural over a nomadic life—the growth of a settled community—is not attained.

Alluvial and Volcanic Soils

There are two most important exceptions to the rule of poor soils in tropical countries. Alluvial soils are fertile and may be found in deposits along lakes, in river valleys, and in deltas. Recent volcanic soils are also usually fertile. Less important, but worthy of mention, forest soils of tropical mountains that are high enough to escape the great heat of lower altitudes may be fertile and rich in humus.

South and southeast Asia are more favored with good soils than

7. Edgar Aubert de la Rüe, François Boulière, and Jean-Paul Harroy write in *The Tropics* (New York: Knopf, 1957), pp. 171–72:

The spectacle is very typical: a few tall trees . . . are still standing. . . . [E]verywhere the stumps are standing, and between them the soft iron hoes of the women scratch the ground to make it produce a few crops of bananas, manioc, or sweet potatoes. Here and there dotting these primitive fields, the untidiest in the world, are the blackened trunks that have not been properly burned. . . . Two or three years, sometimes four, of this exposure of the soil to the sun's rays and to the rains, are enough to deprive it of its fertility, and then the village waits for the signal from its old men and its witch doctors to depart to a new site. . . . The abandoned clearing is then reconquered more or less rapidly by the forest. . . . When sufficient land is available, the seminomadic group, under the leadership of its chiefs, makes ten to fifteen shifts before returning to a spot formerly occupied by it.

any other major area with a tropical climate. The great rivers in this area bring down much of the soluble plant food that has been removed from the soils upstream in the catchment area. Much of this better soil derives from outside the Tropics proper, where different processes control the formation of soils. Despite these advantages, some areas in south and southeast Asia—notably the coastal plains in eastern Sumatra, western and southern Borneo and southwestern New Guinea—suffer the drawbacks of vast swamps. Waterlogged soil inhibits bacterial action, dead vegetation accumulates at the surface, and the potential fertility of these areas remains unused. Elsewhere, in large areas of Indonesia such as eastern and central Java, much of Bali and Lombok, and some spots in Sumatra and Celebes, plus scattered parts of the Philippines and the Deccan plateau base of Bombay in India, the soil has been formed from volcanic eruptions and may be very rich.

Tropical Africa's largest areas of alluvial soil are south of Lake Albert and Lake Kioga in Uganda and between the Blue and White Nile in Sudan. Volcanic soils are found in Rwanda, Burundi, western Cameroon, and Ethiopia; central Kenya and Tanzania extending from Mt. Meru to Mt. Kilimanjaro; the Kipengere Mountains at the head of Lake Malawi; and Mt. Elgon and the Ruwenzori Mountains in Uganda.

In the Americas, fertile volcanic soil is present on some of the Caribbean islands (for example, Guadeloupe and Martinique) and in parts of Mexico, Costa Rica, and Colombia. The Amazon has only a narrow flood plain of good soil; the rest of the basin has mostly poor laterite soil.

Protein Supply

The composition of soils over most of the Tropics affects the character of the food supply grown. The chemical makeup of tropical soils tends to result in a shortage of protein in the diet—a nutritional shortage that has an impact on work efficiency:

> As might be expected, tropical plants tend to be poor in nitrogeneous constituents which must be manufactured from the precarious supplies in the soil. On the other hand they are relatively rich in carbohydrate which can be synthesized by the plant from carbon dioxide in the air and the abundant water. Sugar, manioc, rice, corn . . . sweet potatoes [and ba-

nanas and plantains] are familiar examples of tropical foodstuffs rich in carbohydrate but relatively poor in protein.[8]

Protein is the critical nutrient for physical and mental growth and
its shortage may be a major factor inhibiting development. Considerable evidence further indicates a relation between malnutrition of
children, mainly in the form of protein shortages, and mental retardation. Alan D. Berg, senior nutrition adviser at the World Bank,
suggests that malnourished children may be basically dull. If true,
the relation suggests a significant problem for those children—as
many as two-thirds of the children of most developing countries—
who are now suffering some degree of malnutrition.[9] The chain of
evidence is still quite fragile, but it does appear possible that the
peculiar composition of tropical soils has had a substantial impact
on the pace of development in passing along a nutritional deficiency
to humans that in turn impedes both their physical and their mental
development.

8. Lee, *Climate and Economic Development in the Tropics*, p. 33. D. J.
Parsons and Don Stoops of the World Bank staff, commenting on this book,
point out that some leguminous crops that synthesize their own nitrogen are
high-protein crops and can be grown under tropical conditions. The Common-
wealth Scientific and Industrial Research Organization in Queensland has developed tropical legumes that are commercially viable in Australia.

9. "Malnutrition and National Development," *Foreign Affairs* 46 (October
1967), p. 126.

4. Agricultural Enemies

The locusts were falling like hail on to the roof . . . It sounded like a heavy storm. . . . Looking out, all the trees were queer and still, clotted with insects, their boughs weighed to the ground. The earth seemed to be moving, locusts crawling everywhere.

DORIS LESSING, *African Stories*

Tropical conditions, as indicated in the preceding chapters, foster the multiplication of species and subspecies that attack agriculture. D. H. K. Lee has pointed out that any attempt to introduce or expand output of a particular crop increases the dangers associated with these preying species. Not only does such introduction or expansion run the risk of rapid multiplication among the wide variety of existing predators but it may also encourage the activation or evolution of a new set of predators.

Research in this field apparently has not yet produced anything approaching a systematic summation of the economic impact of the diseases and pests that afflict agriculture in the Tropics. I have not found any comprehensive analysis of this set of obstacles to agricultural development either in technical books on tropical agriculture or in books on economic development problems. The best coverage is clearly on diseases of animals. The closest thing to a summation of research results is that prepared in the U.S. government for the President's Science Advisory Committee for livestock:

Animal diseases constitute one of the most important limitations to the development of more productive livestock industries. Epizootic diseases capable of killing or debilitating large population of animals are largely uncontrolled in developing countries [and yet] the greatest total loss results not from the

30

spectacular epizootic diseases, but from the many parasitic, infectious, nutritional, toxic, metabolic, and organic diseases that affect livestock . . . especially in developing countries . . . Accurate data are not available on the incidence or prevalence of various livestock diseases in developing countries, but there is no doubt that it is great. . . . Because most developing countries are in the tropics or subtropics, most of the livestock disease problems . . . are significantly different from those of developed countries located in temperate climates. Although many principles of medical science and disease control developed for temperate regions apply to tropical problems, there is a critical deficiency in knowledge of tropical veterinary medicine.[1]

The U.S. National Academy of Sciences comments in *Tropical Health* that intestinal parasites occur in nearly all domestic animals throughout the Tropics. The economic effects, notes the Academy, are not necessarily confined to mortality in infected animals:

These parasites are responsible also for retarded development of young animals, reduced yields of milk and meat, lowered wool production, and impaired working capacity of draft animals. . . . [T]ransmission [of gastrointestinal parasites] can and does take place in most instances throughout the year, whereas in the temperate zones low temperatures serve as a barrier to transmission during the winter months.[2]

That same tropical environment that favors the rapid and luxuriant growth of crops and vegetation also nourishes those weeds that compete for moisture and nutrients. Gordon Wrigley, in his standard work on *Tropical Agriculture: The Development of Production*, also notes that without a "close season" for plant growth, all sorts of pests may thrive all the year: not only weeds, but the parasitic fungi, insects, spider mites, eelworms and virus diseases that make for serious reductions in the crops. Even after harvest, serious losses can result from storage pests and rats.

1. William R. Pritchard and others, "Intensification of Animal Production," in President's Science Advisory Committee, *The World Food Problem*, 3 vols. (Washington, D.C.: Government Printing Office, 1967), 2:271.
2. *Tropical Health: A Report on a Study of Needs and Resources* (Washington, D.C.: National Academy of Sciences–National Research Council, 1962), p. 175.

Weeds and Insects

Some enemies may largely wipe out a crop, while others that are not lethal to the plant but nevertheless just as insidious may cause crop damage. For example, Wrigley mentions the loss of rice in Asia from stem borers and "blast"; he also states that the loss of cocoa pods due to a fungus, *Phytophthora Palmivora*, if uncontrolled, may destroy 75 percent of the potential crop where, as in Cameroon, conditions for the disease are ideal. According to 1954 estimates in the British colonies, the loss of crops from fungal disease alone totaled 12 percent of all crops, varying from over 25 percent of the beverage, drug, and spice crops to about 5 percent of the fruits and pulses. Wrigley concludes that, if weeds, insects, and storage pests all take similar tolls, half the potential harvest is being lost.[3]

In *We Don't Know How*, William and Elizabeth Paddock give an excellent graphic description of what this all means at the level of the typical farmer in Latin America's low Tropics:

> [The farmer clears the] land he intends to plant . . . two to five acres—depending on the number of machete swingers in his family . . . [He then] burns over the whole piece of land he is going to plant. [After he plants his corn,] when the rains come, everything . . . bursts forth: . . . every conceivable weed, insect, and pest, along with the corn. . . . Finally the corn approaches maturity. Then come the weevils that begin eating the new kernels. So do the birds. . . . [It is a] miracle that the long-cultivated, burned-over acres produce any corn at all—not to mention the worn-out farmer himself. He probably has a bit of chronic malaria, also some amoeba and a variety of other debilitating "hitchhikers" festering in his system. Nevertheless, . . . the average Guatemalan or Mexican peasant farmer produces twelve bushels to the acre—about what his ancestors produced a thousand years ago. . . . But development planners and politicians and foreign aid men refuse to recognize the poor, worn-out quality of tropical land. Dirt is dirt, they say. There cannot be much difference in it.

The situation is in severe contrast to the Midwest of the United States fifty years ago, before the use of, for example, modern equip-

3. *Tropical Agriculture*, p. 215.

ment, fertilizers, herbicides, and improved seeds. The severe winter was a help because it suppressed weeds and pests. The land produced enough to support the farmer, his family, and a horse. With the horse he could cultivate a bigger piece of land than the tropical farmer. The Paddocks continue:

> When he planted his corn . . . [g]ermination was a slow process for both corn and weeds. This meant that plants grew slowly at first. Thus he could cultivate his fields several times before the soil warmed up, eliminating most of his weeds. By late June, when . . . the plants began growing faster, no further cultivating was necessary because the corn was now high enough to shade out any late-sprouting weeds. . . . [The farmer] did not fertilize fifty years ago, but . . . nutrients had not yet been leached out of the virgin soil. And because of lower temperatures the organic matter was not broken down by soil organisms as it is in the tropics. Even with unimproved seed the Midwest farmer of fifty years ago averaged thirty-two bushels of corn to the acre, two and one-half times as much as the tropical peasant farmer of today. . . . The peasant in the tropics is condemned to poverty as long as he is unable to muster both the capital and the know-how needed to combat successfully the limitations of his land—the weeds, the pests, the lack of soil nutrients.[4]

Researchers estimate that the cost of insect control is around 20 percent of the value of the cotton crop in Colombia and about 45 percent in Nicaragua.[5] To this would also need to be added the losses due to weeds and any diseases of cotton.

Locusts

Among the enduring enemies of agriculture in the Tropics are the locusts.[6] Gigantic swarms of desert locusts can fly over

4. We Don't Know How, pp. 171–73.

5. Philippe Leurquin, "Cotton Growing in Colombia: Achievements and Uncertainties," Food Research Institute Studies 6 (1966), pp. 170–71; and W. W. McPherson and Bruce F. Johnston, "Distinctive Features of Agricultural Development in the Tropics," in Agricultural Development and Economic Growth, p. 208.

6. The best summary and analysis of research findings on locusts is Peter T. Haskell, "Locust Control: Ecological Problems and International Pests," in The

1,900 kilometers nonstop and attack crops anywhere from west Africa to India. The red locust by comparison is limited to southern, central, and eastern Africa. Effective action against either species of locust requires international cooperation. The red locust has been successfully controlled in this way in recent years—the desert locust only partially. But in both cases, control has relied too much on insecticides and now the locusts show signs of growing resistance.

Doris Lessing in her *African Stories* vividly describes what the locusts can do to a farm:

> *The air was darkening. A strange darkness, for the sun was blazing. . . . The locusts were coming fast. Now half the sky was darkened. Behind the reddish veils in front, which were the advance guards of the swarm, the main swarm showed in a dense black cloud, reaching almost to the sun itself. . . . By now the locusts were falling like hail on to the roof of the kitchen. It sounded like a heavy storm. . . . Looking out, all the trees were queer and still, clotted with insects, their boughs weighed to the ground. The earth seemed to be moving, locusts crawling everywhere . . . The rustling of the locust armies was like a big forest in the storm; their settling on the roof was like the beating of the rain; the ground was invisible in the sleek, brown, surging tide—it was like being drowned in locusts, sub-merged by the loathsome brown flood. . . . And now from the trees, from the earth all round them, the locusts were tak-ing wing. . . . A reddish-brown steam was rising off the miles of bush, off the lands, the earth. . . . And as the clotted branches lifted, the weight on them lightening, there was noth-ing but the black spines of branches, trees. . . . The lands which had been filmed with green, the new tender mealie plants, were stark and bare. All the trees stripped. A devastated landscape. No green, no green anywhere.*[7]

The desert locust (*Schistocerca gregaria Forskal*) may breed any-where in the area in north Africa, the southern fringe of the Sahara, the Middle East, Iran, Afghanistan, Pakistan, and India where and when conditions are suitable. The locust requires very little:

Careless Technology: Ecology and International Development, ed. M. Taghi Farver and John P. Milton (Garden City, N.Y.: Doubleday [Natural History], 1972), pp. 499–526.

7. "A Mild Attack of Locusts," in *African Stories* (New York: Simon & Schuster, 1965), pp. 540–41, 543, 545.

bare ground for egg laying, a minimum of moisture and of food. The red locust (*Nomadacris septem-fasciato Serville*) breeds in restricted areas in Tanzania, Zambia, and Malawi. Both the desert and red locusts may appear in truly gigantic swarms—one was measured at 80 kilometers long and 42 kilometers wide (about 50 by 26 miles). In the enormous swarms, locusts may have a combined weight of around 40,000 metric tons, and such a mass of insects can eat as much food in one day as can 10,000 people.

When the density of their population is low, locusts behave like grasshoppers. It is only when their population becomes dense and their physical appearance changes that they become gregarious and operate together. In this phase, while still immature, they are hoppers and can move up to twenty kilometers a day. As adults with wings, they become a flying swarm and can move with the wind as a single entity during weeks of migration over hundreds or thousands of kilometers. In 1952 swarms of the desert locust originating in Ethiopia and Somalia moved thousands of kilometers to breed in a belt extending from Jordan to Pakistan.

Locusts lay their eggs in bare soil. Incubation periods range from less than ten days in hot climates to more than one hundred days in cold climates. Locusts can fly only when their thoracic muscle temperature is 25°C (77°F), so the geographic limits of the swarms correlate with climate. Normally, the locusts produce one new generation a year. The size of the locust population may vary considerably from year to year depending upon whether the weather has been favorable for reproduction and growth. Plagues of desert locusts, when an overlarge population appeared in many swarms, occurred during this century in the 1920s, early 1930s, late 1940s, 1950s, and most recently in 1967, 1968, and 1969. The map on page 36 depicts the locusts' invasion area.

The red locust has been controlled by an independent international organization, the International Red Locust Control Service, which has been maintained by contributions from a number of African countries—Angola, Botswana, Burundi, Kenya, Lesotho, Malawi, Mozambique, Rhodesia, South Africa, Swaziland, Tanzania, Uganda, Zaïre, and Zambia. The Service operates on a small budget amounting for instance in 1967 to only $73,000. Successful control of the locusts in their breeding grounds has been accomplished by aerial chemical spraying. The main danger to this success story is that very little research is being carried on, especially concerning prospects for controlling the red locust by means other than insecticides. If the red locust develops a resistance to insecticides, and it has already

LOCUST INVASIONS

Approximate limits of invasion areas:

--- Desert locust

▨ Red locust

IBRD 12442
October 1976

The boundaries shown on this map do not imply endorsement or acceptance by the World Bank and its affiliates.

KILOMETERS
0   1000   2000   3000
0   1000   2000
MILES

demonstrated some potential to do so, it could again swarm out of control.

The desert locust is a more difficult problem. Although much progress has been made in controlling it, this species is still an important threat throughout its entire invasion area. The desert locust may breed in a vast area, so finding the new swarms before they migrate to attack crops is difficult. In western Africa, locusts breed in July through September. The resultant swarms migrate north to north Africa, where they in turn breed in March through June, then recross the Sahara to feed and breed again. In addition to this north and south cycle, swarms may move east or west within the invasion area. No permanent breeding areas in fact exist. The locust depends on its migrations, which are at least partly initiated and controlled by the weather, to find areas where suitable breeding conditions exist.

The areas in which the locust breeds and migrates cover so many countries that international coordination of information and attacks on the locust swarms is essential. The Food and Agriculture Organization (FAO) in Rome, financed by the United Nations Development Programme, has international responsibility for coordinating action. The FAO organizes international meetings for the purpose and sets up regional commissions to help countries cooperate. Two independent regional organizations cooperate with the FAO: the Organisation Commune de Lutte Anti-acridien et de Lutte Anti-aviare of countries in west Africa, and the Desert Locust Control Organisation for eastern Africa. The FAO also sponsors a locust news summary and forecasting service. This organization, the Desert Locust Information Service, operated out of the British government's Anti-Locust Research Center, collects and disseminates intelligence information that warns of breeding and the formation and migration of swarms so that preventive action can be taken.

The countries cooperating against the desert locust attempt to find and destroy swarms as they are forming. Unfortunately, it has not yet been possible to kill enough desert locusts to eliminate the swarms and "plagues" such as those of 1967, 1968, and 1969. One difficulty is that political factors and insufficient finance have prevented the creation of a centralized service such as that combatting the red locust. The breeding places of the desert locusts are also difficult to find. Unless all countries in which these insects breed carry out the necessary minimum amount of reconnaissance and control, some swarms are bound to escape. Finally, the control measures so far applied, as in the case of the red locust, are dependent on existing insecticides and no more permanent solution has as yet been found.

Trypanosomiasis

Trypanosomiasis is one of the most important obstacles to economic development in Africa.[8] The disease is caused by trypanosomes (a protozoan flagellate), principally carried by the tsetse fly, and takes many forms. Nagana, sleeping sickness, and Chagas' disease are all caused by various protozoans of this genus. Trypanosomiasis prevents much of Africa from progressing beyond subsistence agriculture. For centuries, by killing transport animals, it abetted the isolation of tropical Africa from the rest of the world and the isolation of the various African peoples from one another. The only trade of consequence that could take place over most of the area was in commodities of great value and little bulk—for example, gold and ivory—or in a commodity that was provided with its own legs —that is to say, the slave.

African forms of trypanosomiasis are serious diseases. Most are transmitted through the actual bite of an infected tsetse, which in sucking blood introduces the parasitic trypanosome into the blood. In humans, the parasite eventually enters the nervous system and affects the brain and spinal cord. Unless treatment is obtained, the infected person dies after a period of lethargy. Drugs are now available that can effect a cure, and in some but not all cases innoculation will give temporary protection against infection. Repeated surveys, constant surveillance with mass treatment to eliminate the human reservoirs of the trypanosomes, and avoidance of some areas for settlement, have reduced the incidence of human sleeping sickness to a fairly low level. The mortality rate has been greatly reduced.

Cattle, if only lightly infected by the parasite, can be treated with drugs and cured. However, in vast areas eradication of the disease has not yet proven possible and the density of flies and the disease make the drug treatment for cattle ineffective. The animal disease

8. As Jacques M. May states: "This disease is of great importance and has played a considerable role in keeping central Africa in its present state of backwardness. It is entirely possible that [the inability of] the people of Africa . . . to raise their living standards above the most primitive level has been directly or indirectly related to their relationship with the parasite." See *Studies in Disease Ecology* (New York: Hafner, 1961), p. 231.

has its natural reservoir in the wild animals of Africa, who have built up an immunity to it.

With the coming of mechanical transport, the impact of the tsetse fly with the infectious protozoans it carries has been limited to influencing agriculture and the distribution of the human population. This is still a substantial impact. Over the larger part of tropical Africa, the fly and its transmission of a trypanosomiasis called nagana has prevented the keeping of cattle for food or use as draught animals. Over 10 million square kilometers of Africa—an area greater than that of the United States—are thereby denied to cattle. There are now around 114 million cattle in Africa. If the carrying capacity of the infested area be taken at about 12 cattle per square kilometer (1 every eight hectares, or the present average carrying capacity of land in Africa) the land cleared of the fly could carry an additional 128 million cattle. In other terms, cattle output roughly could double. Since the main food deficiency in Africa is protein, the increased meat supply could also have substantial indirect productive benefits. The ability to use draught cattle in most African farming areas would also mean that cultivation no longer would remain dependent on human muscles and that mixed farming with the use of manure for fertilizer would finally be practicable in most areas.

The tsetse's high density and its additional danger of sleeping sickness infection in humans also prevents habitation and cultivation of some fertile areas. Sleeping sickness, another form of trypanosomiasis, is no longer the acute danger it once was, but the disease is far from being conquered. When sleeping sickness was first introduced into east Africa, between 1902 and 1905, probably carried there by Stanley's expedition from west Africa, the disease killed two-thirds of the 300,000 population in the area north of Lake Victoria. The disease was brought under control only by removing the population from the lake shores. This was the most spectacular example of the power of the disease, but throughout large areas of Africa it had and continues to have an impact on where people can live and on the way they can make their living. The map on page 40 shows the distribution of the disease in the African and American Tropics.

There are twenty-four species of tsetse (genus *Glossina*) in Africa. Each of the species has different habits and requires different types of country to survive, but none can exist on any food other than blood. They are highly susceptible to water loss from the body, particularly where the temperature is high. Lost moisture must be

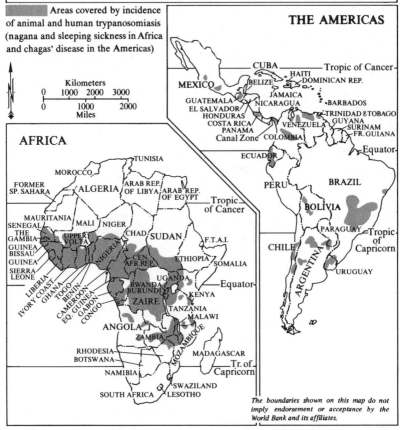

GEOGRAPHICAL DISTRIBUTION OF
ANIMAL AND HUMAN TRYPANOSOMIASIS

IBRD 12443
October 1976

Areas covered by incidence of animal and human trypanosomiasis (nagana and sleeping sickness in Africa and chagas' disease in the Americas)

THE AMERICAS

AFRICA

The boundaries shown on this map do not imply endorsement or acceptance by the World Bank and its affiliates.

replaced from a meal of blood at least every two or three days or the fly dies. Thus, in the Sudan zone across Africa (between the tropical rain forests along the coast and semidesert approaches to the Sahara), where humidity is low and there is little shade, the tsetse survives only in the fringe forests along river banks. Closer to the equator, where acacia and similar trees provide shelter, and in the humid tropical forest zone, the fly can often take over completely. But if human population is sufficiently dense to destroy the tree shelter for the fly, the tsetse may be pushed back and trypanosomiasis may be controlled by drugs. Unfortunately, because of the poverty of African tropical soils, shifting cultivation may be necessary.[9] Allowing cultivated areas thereby to revert to bush fallow to restore

9. See page 27.

the land's fertility re-creates a natural habitat for the fly. Thus, the pattern may be mosaic in nature: tsetse areas scattered in among farming areas, both varying in size according to the fertility of the land and the density of population.

An experiment conducted in Nigeria gives a graphic picture of the impact of the diseases carried by the tsetse. In 1963, twenty-eight Zebu cattle were driven over 400 miles from a tsetse-free area in north Nigeria to Ilorin in the south. The trek took twenty-eight days, through fly country. On arrival, eleven of the herd were found to be infected. They were then held for a seventeen-day observation period. By the end of this period, nineteen of the herd died, eight more were dying and only one still remained in good condition.

The history of efforts to combat the fly is one of constantly fluctuating battle lines. Three main approaches have been to destroy the breeding areas of the fly, by clearing the type of bush it favors; to remove its food supply, shooting out all the game; and to kill the fly with insecticide. When the fly is destroyed in an area, an attempt is made to maintain a fly-free barrier against still infested areas. The fly has shown considerable ingenuity in surviving: it has developed a fondness for traveling by automobile and, unless automobiles coming out of infested areas are cleaned of the fly, it may leapfrog control measures directed against it. As more roads are built in the course of economic development, the danger of the fly's spread also becomes greater.

In some parts of west and central Africa the indigenous N'dama dwarf cattle have some resistance to trypanosomes. There has been some exploration of the idea of developing these cattle for meat production in the tsetse areas. However, the cattle are slow maturing, low meat yielding, and developing them into more efficient animals is likely to take a considerable period of time. Unfortunately, their resistance also tends to be localized against their own particular strains of trypanosomes, and their tolerance to infection tends to break down when they are moved. If no better way of handling the tsetse or the trypanosomes can be found, the solution may have to concentrate on breeding resistance into cattle.

The American form of trypanosomiasis occurs widely throughout South America but is much less important than the African disease. It is usually known as Chagas' disease and results in anemia, swellings, fever, and heart disease. It is transmitted mainly by a species of bed bug and, consequently, Chagas' disease can be prevented by domestic sanitation.

Other Agricultural Evils

Another cattle infection of somewhat lesser importance than nagana is east coast fever, a tick-borne disease. East coast fever kills half a million calves a year in east and central Africa. Since nonlocal, or exotic, breeds of cattle are particularly susceptible to this disease, the disease has inhibited upgrading through crossbreeding. The United Nations Development Programme, the three East African Community partners, and bilateral aid sources in the United Kingdom and United States are financing an intensive effort to find and develop an effective vaccine for cattle.

To round out this parade of pests, one might add a bird and an unusual weed. In Africa a weaverbird, the red-billed *Quelea* finch, occupies the savanna areas across Africa both north and south of the equator. Flocks of tens or hundreds of thousands of weaverbirds often descend on crops when they are ripe and clear them out, thereby forming an important obstacle to any large food-growing project over this immense area of the Tropics.

Weeds usually hurt crops by competing for nutrients and water. But one of the enemies of sorghum, a basic cereal throughout much of Africa, is the purple-flowered witchweed. This weed parasite feeds on the roots of sorghum, thus directly weakening the plant.

5. Agriculture Research

The difference between the set of parameters confronting agriculture in the Tropics and the set in the Temperate Zone is not economically trivial: so far the difference has helped keep people in the Tropics poor. But this may be true largely because existing agricultural technology was developed mainly to handle the problems and characteristics of Temperate Zone agriculture. Some characteristics of the Tropics give tropical agriculture a potential advantage over Temperate Zone agriculture. The U.S. government's presidential Science Advisory Committee report notes that sunlight energy for plant growth in the humid Tropics ranges between 60 and 90 percent higher than that available in humid temperate regions. These values fully discount offsetting effects of considerable cloudiness in the Tropics, as well as seasonal limitations modified by daylength in temperate regions.[1] David B. Grigg writes that plants in tropical rain forests produce as much as three to five times more organic matter each year than do plants in temperate forests.[2] He adds that the absence of winter, once pests are controlled, can extend the length of the growing season. The multiplicity of species could help in developing new and better crops and livestock.

Livestock

According to World Bank livestock experts, a principal technical reason for the low levels of livestock productivity stems

1. *The World Food Problem*, p. 2:490.
2. *The Harsh Lands*, p. 214.

directly from the tropical climate itself. Once understood, this problem can be handled. The low productivity is due mainly to the wide seasonal fluctuations in the growth and quality of pastureland, caused by the alternating wet and dry seasons in large parts of the Tropics. Because these areas lack stock watering facilities, the number of animals that can be safely carried through the dry season is the maximum that can be carried for the whole year. Moreover, much of the weight that the livestock gain during the wet season when feed is plentiful is lost when feed is short, so the average yearly weight gain is very low. Long periods of underfeeding lower the reproduction rates of the herd, and increase susceptibility to parasitic and other diseases. By providing fences, water, and corrals, which are essential for grazing management and controlling disease, it is possible to achieve triple and even greater increases in production. In addition, pastures can be improved by using a number of new legume plants that fix nitrogen in the soil and that have been developed for the tropical areas of Australia in Queensland.[3]

Crops

The dominant leitmotiv emerging in agriculture is the need for research into means of coping with tropical obstacles and turning some tropical characteristics into assets. Today's comparatively advanced state of agriculture in the Temperate Zones took many years to achieve. Although the techniques and solutions to Temperate Zone problems cannot be transferred automatically to the Tropics, much of the basic theoretical approach is likely to be valid. The approach to soil problems evolved in recent years is summed up by Charles E. Kellogg as a realization that soils are "dynamic and changing." Soils support living plants and microorganisms that in turn have much to do with the formation and behavior of the soils. Soil is a physical and biological as well as a chemical and geological system.[4] The most efficient systems of soil

3. J. M. Fransen and others, "World Bank Lending for Livestock Development," restricted circulation memorandum of the Agriculture and Rural Development Department, World Bank (Washington, D.C., October 1971), pp. 5–6.

4. "We Seek; We Learn," in Soil, The Yearbook of Agriculture (Washington, D.C.: Government Printing Office, 1957), p. 8.

management, Kellogg feels, are combinations of practices, fitted to unique soils to realize benefits from the many interactions among soil processes and characteristics.[5]

Until very recently, there has been little research on tropical agricultural problems other than on some export crops and, most recently, on tropical wheat and rice.[6] Appreciable research effort on a few export crops and fertilizer essentially began only after World War II. Earlier beginnings, after World War I, were crippled by the depression of the 1930s and World War II. The drive to independence, then, had as an unfortunate by-product a substantial drop or cession in research effectiveness in many areas, particularly in Africa as expatriates left and qualified Africans found better opportunities in government offices, politics, and private enterprise. Although southeast Asia has been favored in the quality of its alluvial soils, comparatively little has been done to understand the soils better and improve their quality by deliberate human effort. The dominant wet-rice farming system has taken advantage of the fact that the rice takes little from the soil—the water covering the soil comes from the upper courses of the rivers and contains many valuable plant foods, so it helps to reduce the rate at which plant nutrients are removed from the soil.[7]

Since World War II experiments with fertilizer and plant breeding in tree crops have produced remarkably good results in productivity and improved plants. But fertilizers are expensive and little is known about which specific soil deficiencies need to be corrected or how they *can* be corrected. It took some twenty years, for example, to discover what essential trace elements (tiny percentages of, for example, zinc, boron, copper, and cobalt) had to be added to the soils and what other adaptations to African conditions were needed to raise non-African breeds of livestock successfully.

Research in east Africa has shown that, in some circumstances, shifting cultivation can be modified by replacing the bush fallow with a grass ley that can be grazed by livestock as a productive part of land rotation. This makes it possible to maintain soil fertility

5. Ibid., p. 10.

6. McPherson and Johnston write: "The universities of Latin America, established a hundred years or so before the first one of the United States, only recently began to work in research and education oriented toward the problems of agriculture and rural people." See *Agricultural Development and Economic Growth*, p. 214.

7. Fisher, *South-east Asia*, p. 53.

without using fertilizers under both grazing and nongrazing regimes.[8]

One ingenious way governments have found to cut losses from pests is to impose an artificial winter. Many cotton-growing countries in the Tropics and sub-Tropics legislate a dead season by setting a date when the crop must be uprooted and burned and setting a date when planting may begin.

Over the last seventy years a combination of techniques has been developed to improve agricultural productivity in the temperate climates. In brief, biological engineering has learned how to create new varieties of plants tailored to a set of planned characteristics, adapted to take advantage of favorable climatic and soil characteristics and avoid unfavorable ones. The plants are bred to convert large amounts of fertilizer into a usable product rather than to excessive foliage. Research has also devised ways of building into new varieties high response to intensive management. Low yields from old varieties often made the use of protectants against pests and insects uneconomic. Using these protectants on high-yield varieties, however, may pay extremely well. Research has taught us that resistance to pests and diseases may even be bred into plants. When yields are increased in this way, specially designed farm machinery for a particular crop may then become economic.

This "package of techniques" approach has evolved slowly in the industrialized countries and, until recently, it was not applied to the tropical countries. The experience of the Rockefeller Foundation in developing the high-yield Mexican dwarf wheat and that of the International Rice Research Institute in developing high-yield rice has shown that the package approach to tropical agriculture can promote yields in the Tropics at least as high as those in temperate climates. The average yield of a commodity can be rapidly increased through application of a complete package of high-yielding varieties; appropriate fertilizer appropriately used; adequate disease and pest control; proper planting, cultivation, and irrigation techniques; and in the case of animals, the right breed, nutrition, and management.

On the one hand, this "package of techniques" approach can offset the poverty of tropical soils through fertilizer and offset the unsatisfactorily erratic rainfall through irrigation and drainage. On the other hand, this approach can take advantage of the heat and absence of frost to produce two or three crops a year. Research has developed

8. Dennis J. Parsons, "Climate and Economic Development," restricted circulation memorandum of the South Asia Regional Department, World Bank (Washington, D.C., May 1973), p. 2.

a biological key to knowledge of how to put together sets of practices for tropical conditions that lack in the strictly biological assets for increased production.[9]

The dramatic accomplishments of research in developing high-yield varieties of tropical rice, wheat, and corn, the basis of the so-called Green Revolution, are examples of the kind of payoff research on tropical agriculture might be able to make. The Rockefeller and Ford Foundations, which sponsored and financed this research, in 1968 organized two more institutes on tropical agriculture in Colombia and Nigeria to work towards comprehensive development of the agriculture of the lowland tropics. In 1971, an International Potato Center was established in Peru.

A Consultative Research Group

An important step forward was taken in 1971 with the formation of the Consultative Group on International Agricultural Research (CGIAR), jointly sponsored by the Food and Agriculture Organization of the United Nations (FAO), the World Bank, and the United Nations Development Programme (UNDP). The Consultative Group establishes priorities for an expanded international agricultural research program on problems of the less developed countries and mobilizes and coordinates financial support for such a program. The financial resources made available have grown rapidly, from $15 million at the beginning in 1971 to $64 million in 1976.

The Consultative Group's main objectives include examination of the needs of developing countries for special effort in agricultural research on food crops. CGIAR works on international and regional levels in critical subjects otherwise not likely to be adequately covered by existing research facilities. The Group considers how those needs could be met, and tries to assure the greatest possible complementarity of international and regional efforts with national efforts in the financing and the undertaking of agricultural research. CGIAR encourages the exchange of information among research centers at all three levels. Another main objective of the Consultative Group is to review financial and other requirements of international and regional research activities which the Group considers of high priority, and to consider the provision of finance for these, taking account of the

9. *The World Food Problem*, p. 2:491.

need to ensure continuity of research over a substantial period. CGIAR continually reviews priorities and research networks related to developing countries' needs and suggests feasibility studies of specific proposals, to promote agreement on how to undertake and finance them and exchange information on their results.

In addition to the World Bank, FAO, UNDP, and United Nations Environmental Program, the Consultative Group's January 1976 membership included the African Development Bank, Inter-American Development Bank, Asian Development Bank, International Development Research Centre of Canada, Ford Foundation, Kellogg Foundation, Rockefeller Foundation, and the governments of Australia, Belgium, Canada, Denmark, France, the Federal Republic of Germany, Iran, Italy, Japan, the Netherlands, New Zealand, Nigeria, Norway, Saudi Arabia, Sweden, Switzerland, the United Kingdom, and the United States, plus representatives from developing countries in five regions of the world (Africa, Asia and the Far East, Latin America, the Middle East, and southern and eastern Europe), designated for a two-year term by the membership of FAO. Some other OPEC members (Organization of Petroleum Exporting Countries) have expressed growing interest in CGIAR and will probably become contributors in the future. The World Bank acts as chairman and provides the secretariat for CGIAR.

The Consultative Group is advised by a Technical Advisory Committee, chaired by Sir John Crawford of Australia and composed of thirteen experts with broad experience in the agricultural problems of developing countries.[10] This committee is responsible for advising CGIAR on the principal gaps in agricultural research and on the international and regional programs that deserve financial priority.

The Technical Advisory Committee reviews research programs currently under way in the world and considers proposals for several new research centers to meet needs as they are identified. As of early 1976, twelve major international centers and programs were being supported by CGIAR, covering all the major foodstuffs and livestock and all the ecological zones of the developing countries in the Tropics and sub-Tropics.

10. As this book went to press, Sir John Crawford retired from his post after a tenure of some five years. He will be succeeded by Ralph Cummings, Sr., director of the International Crops Research Institute for the Semi-Arid Tropics.

International Research Centers

Centro Internacional de Mejoramiento de Maíz y Trigo (CIMMYT) in Mexico has the responsibility for increasing the quantity and quality of maize and wheat production, and has made an advance of great importance in developing high-yield varieties of these crops. CIMMYT is finding, from tests under conditions that prevail on many small farms, that the new, high-yield varieties are also more efficient than other varieties in their use of fertilizer and water at levels of inputs that small farmers are likely to be able to afford. CIMMYT is breeding and testing maize of superior protein content, and is developing a shorter maize plant which can be planted more densely than the old, tall varieties, with a corresponding increase in yield of 100 percent or more. CIMMYT also has begun work on crossbreeds of winter wheats, which have superior drought tolerance, and spring wheats, which have superior resistance to disease. Field trials of these crosses so far have been encouraging.

The International Rice Research Institute (IRRI) in the Philippines has the primary responsibility for research to increase the quantity and quality of rice production. IRRI's development of high-yield varieties of rice is well known. The Institute is making steady progress toward the development of high-yield varieties that will have other attributes as well: a short growing season, a wide spectrum of resistance to diseases, and attractive grain appearance. The Institute also is continuing work in developing systems of interplanting and multiple cropping, centered mostly on rice, which both make maximum use of land and growing seasons and have demonstrated a potential for markedly increasing farm production. Most notable in the Institute's current plans is the inauguration of a special program of research to benefit small farmers by developing seeds and technologies which will increase the production of upland rice, grown without controlled irrigation and usually with meager amounts of fertilizer.

The International Potato Center (CIP) in Peru completed its physical plant and basic staffing in 1974. In the meantime, CIP has made useful progress in screening and adding to its collection of genetic material, and has identified potato varieties which may enable the Center to breed strains highly resistant to blight, the most destructive disease of potatoes in all latitudes.

Four other centers, the International Institute of Tropical Agriculture (IITA) in Nigeria, Centro Internacional de Agricultura Tropical (CIAT) in Colombia, the International Crops Research Institute for the Semi-Arid Tropics (ICRISAT) in India, and the International Center for Agricultural Research in Dry Areas (ICARDA) in Lebanon, Iran, and Syria, are all "comprehensive" institutes. Each directs its research not only to the improvement of specific lines of agricultural production, but also to the improvement of systems of agricultural production—for example, crop rotation, cropping patterns, cultivation practices, and market relations.

Both Centro Internacional de Agricultura Tropical and the International Institute of Tropical Agriculture are concerned with the humid, lowland Tropics, each with emphasis on its own particular region. A particular challenge to IITA is to develop agricultural practices to replace the shifting, bushfallow type of agriculture characteristic of much of Africa. In crops, CIAT has primary responsibility among the centers for field beans and cassava; it also has a program directed at improving the output of beef and swine. IITA has primary responsibility for certain grain legumes (chiefly cowpeas) and for selected roots and tubers (especially sweet potatoes and yams); it does adaptive work on cassava material provided by CIAT. Both CIAT and IITA do adaptive work on IRRI rice and CIMMYT maize. Among the chief accomplishments of the two centers is the demonstration that great gains can be made in their respective regions through the use of new, IRRI-based rice varieties. IITA's work in grain legumes, which have high protein content but a low yield per hectare, is regarded as particularly promising.

The International Crops Research Institute for the Semi-Arid Tropics is the center that will place the most emphasis on dryland farming, the predominant type of cultivation in developing countries. ICRISAT's ecological zone is the semiarid tropics, lying mostly in southern Asia, western Africa and eastern South America; it seeks to develop cereals and legumes of importance in these regions: sorghum, millet, pigeonpeas, and chickpeas. ICRISAT is in its developmental stage. The Center has begun its research and is concentrating its attention on planning and on establishing contacts with other research enterprises in its ecological zone.

The International Center for Agricultural Research in Dry Areas, agreed on in 1975, is the last of the big centers to be planned by the Consultative Group. ICARDA will do research on barley, lentils, farming systems centered on sheep, and the other problems of areas with low and irregular rainfall. Three principal stations serve ICARDA—one each in Lebanon, Iran, and Syria.

Research on livestock in tropical Africa is to be undertaken at the International Livestock Center for Africa (ILCA) in Ethiopia while livestock diseases will be studied at the International Laboratory for Research on Animal Diseases (ILRAD) in Kenya. Both ILCA and ILRAD were still being organized in early 1976.

An International Board for Plant Genetic Resources is being established in Rome to support and coordinate the creation of a network of plant gene collections. The Board aims to conserve characteristics that may be of value in breeding plants with higher yields, better food value, or greater resistance to pests and diseases. Also in Rome, the Consultative Group supports the Current Agricultural Research Information Service and the International Information System for the Agricultural Sciences and Technology. International support has likewise been mobilized for the West African Rice Development Association in Liberia, which will carry out a coordinated program of rice trials to determine those varieties most suited to west Africa.

It is hard to overstate the importance for economic development of this new Consultative Group and its Technical Advisory Committee. For the first time, worldwide priority has been given to establish and support research on the special agricultural problems of food crops in the developing world. Cash investments involved are comparatively modest—$64 million in 1976, probably rising to $100 million a year by the early 1980s—but in terms of development impact, the payoff should be immense. This decision may well rank in history as one of the most significant in the last third of the twentieth century in helping the developing world cope with its particular special problems.

————•••————

The international research effort will not by itself be enough. Individual countries and different regions must apply the results, and this will necessitate additional local adaptive research. Research is generally underrated by developing countries. Money spent on research is not as politically attractive as money spent on showy buildings or prestige projects. Economic planners neglect research because in conventional national accounting it is not regarded as "investment." [11] International aid agencies in the past also have not

11. See Andrew M. Kamarck, " 'Capital' and 'Investment' in Developing Countries," *Finance & Development* 8 (June 1971), pp. 2–9.

given a high priority to research. In this regard, another important policy step was taken in 1969. As the result of a World Bank study on international commodity problems requested by France and fourteen African nations, the Bank decided to consider financing agricultural research facilities, as appropriate, in the developing countries. So far only three comprehensive programs of this type have been worked out and approved for finance. These were in Indonesia, Malaysia, and Spain, where the World Bank is helping finance a comprehensive restructuring and expansion of the agricultural research institutions. Similar programs in early 1976 were being prepared in Brazil, Mexico, and Ecuador. Nepal, Thailand, and Venezuela were also considering this type of program.

Less spectacular but also important in its cumulative effect has been the increasing inclusion of provisions for particular applied agricultural research in World Bank agricultural projects. By May 1975 such provision had been made in more than 100 agricultural projects in 50 countries. For example, in the February 1972 credit for the Zou-Borgou cotton project in Benin (then Dahomey), it was agreed that the project would include four research programs: determination of optimum nutrient application in cotton cultivation and replacement of DDT and Endrin by less "hard" insecticides; introduction and selection of high-yield rice varieties and fertilizer trials on swamp and upland rice; introduction of high yield and disease resistant groundnut varieties and determination of their nutrient requirements; and introduction of new maize and sorghum hybrids and determination of their nutrient requirements.

While the international community still has a long way to go in finding the most effective ways of meeting the problems of agriculture in the Tropics, at least now, in 1976, one can be confident that we are beginning to know much better how to identify the real problems and that we are better organized to find the answers.

6. Minerals

One of the most effective ways in which a poor country can rapidly increase its foreign exchange earnings, government revenues, and investment is through the discovery and exploitation of some rich mineral resource. As UN Secretary-General Kurt Waldheim has pointed out, "most of the countries so far identified as 'least developed' are resource-poor countries or[,] to be more accurate, countries without known exploitable resources."[1] As countries become more industrialized, possession of exploitable mineral resources becomes less important. But for poor countries, possession or lack of such resources may be extremely significant in determining the pace of their growth.[2]

There does not appear to be any rational basis for supposing that countries in the Tropics should have poorer or fewer mineral resources than countries in the Temperate Zones. However, a relatively

1. United Nations, Economic and Social Council, "The International Development Strategy: First Over-all Review and Appraisal of Issues and Policies," Preliminary Report (E/AC.54/L.60), April 1973, p. 33.

2. Hollis B. Chenery, "Land: The Effect of Resources on Economic Growth," in *Economic Development with Special Reference to East Asia*, ed. Kenneth Berrill (New York: St. Martin's, 1964), p. 49. See also Hollis B. Chenery and Lance Taylor, "Development Patterns: Among Countries and Over Time," *The Review of Economics and Statistics* 50 (November 1968): 391–416; this econometric study concluded that, at least among small countries, natural resources differences have a major impact on growth rates even though "[t]here is no single criterion for classifying countries according to resource endowments that is statistically feasible and theoretically satisfactory" (p. 396).

small portion of the world's nonfuel mineral resources has in fact been found so far in the tropical countries. Claude Isbister summarized the reasons for this in terms of the low priority given the search for these minerals in the developing countries:

> [F]irst, big investors have preferred to operate under stable governments and laws; second, the economically developed countries tend to be in Temperate Zones where rock formations are well exposed, and it is only in the past twenty or twenty-five years that prospecting techniques have advanced from surface probing to coping with the third dimension of depth. Many of the developing countries are in tropical and subtropical areas of the world where mineral formations are overburdened by soil.[3]

According to a World Bank study, the developed market economies have almost twice the nonfuel mineral reserves the developing countries have in relation to their area. In relation to population, the developed market economies are more than twice as well off.[4] The table profiles the distribution of population, land area, and mineral reserves for developing and developed markets and the centrally planned economies. Values of estimated mineral reserves are given as weighted averages of all those minerals with reserves (valued at the commonly accepted point of transfer) of more than $1,000 million:

Region	Population	Area (percentage of world total)	Value of estimated mineral reserves
Developing market	50	49	38
Developed market	19	26	35
Centrally planned	31	25	27
Total	100	100	100

Estimates of reserves have well-known problems connected with them. For a mineral deposit to be classified as a reserve it must be economically exploitable. The magnitude of reserves may depend then on such influences as changes in prices, taxation, and technol-

---

3. "Comments on 'Sector Program Paper—The Non Fuel Mineral Industry' " (memorandum of the Executive Directors, World Bank, January 1974), p. 1.

4. World Bank, "The Non Fuel Mineral Industry," restricted circulation sector working paper of the Industrial Projects Department, World Bank (November 1973), pp. 14–15.

ogy. Then, too, companies usually prove only sufficient reserves for the medium term; mineral discoveries are not immediately announced; and "strategic" mineral reserves are often kept confidential, as is also much information on mineral reserves in countries with centrally planned economies. Figures on reserves in the table are only indicative, therefore, but they do suggest that in this sector, as in agriculture, the less developed countries are confronted with greater difficulties in getting economic development going than the presently industrialized countries had.

The additional technical problems of finding minerals in the Tropics as compared to the Temperate Zones have been discussed by the U.S. Geological Survey in an analysis prepared for USAID. The main points are as follows: First, the geophysical and geochemical techniques available for securing knowledge about the basic geology of areas were for the most part developed and tested for conditions in the Temperate Zones. But the physical and chemical parameters of the humid Tropics are different, so the interpretation of the data secured consequently needs a different structure of reference.[5] Even the instruments used may have to be different from those developed for Temperate Zones since extremes of heat and moisture "quickly ruin much of the sensitive instrumentation available today."[6] Conventional prospecting techniques used for many centuries in Temperate Zones also have been less successful in the humid Tropics.

The U.S. Geological Survey analysis points out that base-metal deposits in temperate, semiarid, and arid zones are far more easily located. In the humid Tropics, the rains and high temperatures help rapid weathering—the formation of laterite soils and other soil mantles that "effectively hide the underlying rocks."[7] Also, minerals such as dolomite, limestone, gypsum, and salts of potassium and sodium are relatively soluble and "are most difficult to locate in high rainfall areas."[8] The result is that most of the mineral deposits that are found and exploited are the surface concentrations formed from the weathering action of the climate—for example, bauxite, some iron ores, manganese and nickel, tin, and diamond placers— which consequently can be more easily found.

5. U.S. Agency for International Development, *The Application of Geochemical, Botanical, Geophysical, and Remote Sensing Mineral Prospecting Techniques to Tropical Areas*, Report TA/OST 72-13 (Washington, D.C., November 1972), pp. 4–5.

6. Ibid., p. 54.

7. Ibid., p. 3.

8. Ibid., p. 4.

While in some of the arid Tropics the problems may be no different from those of the arid Temperate Zones, the U.S. Geological Survey in another study concludes that: "One of the most intractable problems faced in mineral exploration is posed by areas formerly possessed of a humid tropic climate but now through climatic change brought to an arid regime. Countries along the southern edge of the Sahara present classic examples of the conditions." [9]

It was not until very recently that the international community recognized a need for special help to the less developed countries in their exploration for minerals. In December 1973 a UN Revolving Fund for Natural Resources Exploration was created to offer such assistance. In June 1975, the UN Development Programme (UNDP) agreed on the operational shape of the new fund and appointed a director. Organization and money-raising proceed apace in 1976. Initial resources amount to around $5 million; another $5 million is in sight for 1977. At the outset, the new UN fund will only accept projects to explore for solid minerals. Regular UNDP programs rather than the new fund will provide assistance for broad geological surveys and training or institutional building.

If successfully launched, the Revolving Fund for Resources Exploration will be the potential center for action to develop knowledge, techniques, and instruments that can be adapted to the problems of finding mineral resources in the Tropics. It is a useful beginning in coping with this particular important problem of the tropical countries.

---

9. R. L. Erickson, "Summary Proposals for Investigations of Techniques in Mineral Exploration Suited to the Special Needs of Tropical Regions," memorandum of the Geological Survey, U.S. Interior Department (January 1974), p. 9.

7. Health Hazards

The true "wealth of nations" is the health of its individuals.

IRVING FISHER

We live under the tyranny of the tropics, paying heavy toll every moment for the barest right of existence. The heat, the damp, the unspeakable fecundity of minute life feeding upon big life . . .

RABINDRANATH TAGORE

Recent economic literature reflects an amazing lack of consideration of the impact of disease on economic development. Even in so comprehensive a collection of essays as *Agricultural Development and Economic Growth*, D. M. Hegsted pointed out that "this volume has not considered the general problems of public health, sanitation and medical care. Ill people are obviously poor and inefficient producers . . . Land use and agricultural development may be determined by parasitic and infectious diseases." [1]

It is probably entirely justified for most economists working on problems of the more developed countries to ignore the economic impact of human disease—it can be assumed that the average economic man is healthy and is in full command of his body and mind and that sickness, though not insignificant, is not normally a major factor in the growth and functioning of the economy. But this assumption is false in today's less developed countries in the Tropics. Exactly the opposite assumption is more likely to be true. Lack of good health affects a person's attitude toward work, initiative, creativity, learning ability, energy, and capacity for heavy or sustained work or thought. In the less developed countries a person who has not been or is not being substantially affected by poor health is the exception.

It is possible that, aside from sustaining an environment favorable

1. "Comment," in *Agricultural Development and Economic Growth*, p. 362.

57

to disease, the tropical climates also have a direct adverse impact on work efficiency, creativity, and initiative of humans and so, in this respect, are still another handicap to the economic growth of the less developed countries. In his pioneering work, D. H. K. Lee concludes that "the problem of possible levels of activity has not been adequately studied, at least with the objectivity that science requires." [2] Lee believes that loss of mental initiative is probably the most important single direct result of exposure to tropical environment. While accuracy may be noticeably affected in the test results of poorly motivated persons, it is relatively unaffected in others except under extreme or unusual conditions.[3] In the nearly twenty years since Lee's book there has been but little further work on the subject. In 1962 the U.S. National Academy of Sciences did report:

> *Laboratory studies on human performance in hot conditions show that there is a deterioration in performance somewhere between 81°F and 86°F effective temperature. [But] the tasks used in laboratory hot rooms are synthetic compared with those in industrial work and the social-psychological relationships of the subjects of the experiments are quite artificial.*[4]

In 1970 Neville Billington, director of the British Heating and Ventilation Research Association, detailed some research results concerning human output and temperature ranges in a paper he titled "Human Performance":

Testing organization	Work	Temperature range in degrees Celsius	Change in output	Percentage of change for each degree Celsius
New York Commission on Ventilation	Weight-lifting	20–24	−15	−4
Schweisheimer	Various tasks	about 27	−3 to −10	−2
Hasse	Mining	18–30	−25	−2
Mackworth	Telegraphy	26–36	—	−2

It appears that a threshold temperature exists, varying for different jobs, and that, above this, increases in temperature bring about decreases in production.[5]

2. *Climate and Economic Development in the Tropics*, p. 100.
3. Ibid.
4. *Tropical Health*, p. 385.
5. G. W. Reynolds [Colt International Limited] to A. M. Kamarck, May 30, 1973, Economic Development Institute, World Bank, Washington, D.C.

Basically, the problem with this subject is that there has been very little research on it and what there is has been done mostly on people in temperate climates, working under hot conditions. Even casual observation shows that productivity may suffer when a person is too hot—or too cold. The very existence of air-conditioning and space heating in homes, offices, and factories serves to prove this. What has not been demonstrated is that economic activity (outside of agriculture) in hot climates where air-conditioning is regarded as necessary is handicapped compared to activity in temperate climates where heating is necessary in winter. But agriculture is not air-conditioned and in most developing countries agriculture is the predominant economic sector. If tropical climates as such do adversely affect human productivity, initiative, and creativity, this would slow down the pace of economic growth in the tropical countries as long as agriculture remains an important activity.

A large number of factors influence the health of a population. Over the developing countries, as a whole, the most important causes of poor health undoubtedly, to my mind, stem from the prevailing poverty. Except in a few instances—perhaps river blindness in areas of western Africa—the argument cannot be made that the tropical climate is the decisive factor in this reinforcing relation between disease and poverty. But there is sufficient evidence that tropical climates make the problem of sickness sufficiently more difficult to handle to warrant the conclusion that less developed countries in the Tropics have a harder task in this regard than countries in the Temperate Zones. This then is another reason why developing countries in the Tropics may lag behind in the world process of economic development.

The difference in average life expectancy at birth in the less developed countries, 49 years, and in the industrialized countries, 70.4 years, indicates the differences in health conditions between the two areas.[6] But it does not sufficiently bring home the fact that the population in the developing countries typically have to adjust to living with disease. To illustrate: in Colombia, 89 percent of the individuals sampled in an intensive nutritional study were infested with some form of parasites; in Peru only 9 out of 122 men sampled in the armed forces had no parasitic infection; autopsy records in

6. Timothy King and others, *Population Policies and Economic Development: A World Bank Staff Report* (Baltimore: Johns Hopkins University Press, 1974), p. 170. See also World Bank, *The Assault on World Poverty: Problems of Rural Development, Education, and Health* (Baltimore: Johns Hopkins University Press, 1975), pp. 348–50.

some areas of east Africa indicate that more than 90 percent of the persons examined were harboring beef tapeworms.[7] John D. Thomas has written that human beings are more heavily parasitized in the African continent than in any other part of the world, with on average two infections per man. Schistosomiasis is the dominant infection, affecting nearly half the population.[8] A study of six villages in the northeast of Brazil found the average person harbored two species of parasitic diseases and the hemoglobin content of his blood was less than half of what is medically regarded as normal.[9] On Ukara Island in Lake Victoria, Tanzania, only 0.6 percent of the population was found free of parasitic infection. Of adults over 40 years, the infection rates were 38 percent for hookworm, 38 percent for bilharzia, and 37 percent for filariasis.[10]

Research studies by a World Bank team in Indonesia found that of the workers on three construction sites tested 84 to 87 percent had hookworm, 50 to 67 percent had roundworm (*Ascaris*), and 44 to 58 percent had whipworm (*Trichiuris trichura*). Of the workers on the plantation sites tested, 88 percent had hookworm, 49 percent had roundworm, and 63 percent had whipworm. These infections resulted in iron deficiency anemia in at least 45 percent of the adult male workers, whose output was around 20 percent lower than that of nonanemic workers.[11] Helminth (intestinal worm) infestation rates in children six years old were 95 percent in Sri Lanka, 97 percent in Bangladesh, and 93 percent in Venezuela.

The greater incidence of disease in tropical compared to temperate climates stems from three basic sets of circumstances. First, tropical countries are subject to the diseases of the Temperate Zones and have in addition some diseases that the temperate countries do

7. Marguerite C. Burk and Mordecai Ezekiel, "Food and Nutrition in Developing Economics," in *Agricultural Development and Economic Growth*, p. 340.

8. "Some Preliminary Observations on the Ecology of a Small Man-made Lake in Tropical Africa," in *Ecology and Economic Development in Tropical Africa*, ed. David Brokensha (Berkeley: University of California Institute of International Studies, 1965), p. 133.

9. Mentioned by Dieter Koch-Weser [Harvard Medical School] in the course of a discussion in November 1971.

10. William Laurie, "Survey before Service: Observations on Relations between Agriculture, Parasite Load, and Nutrition on a Tropical African Island," *The Lancet* 2 (October 16, 1954), pp. 801–02.

11. Samir S. Basta and Anthony Churchill, "Iron Deficiency Anemia and the Productivity of Adult Males in Indonesia," Staff Working Paper no. 175 (Washington D.C.: World Bank, April 1974), pp. 18, 29, 39.

not. Next, the Tropics offer more hospitable conditions for some diseases than do the Temperate Zones. For example, most vector-borne diseases are easier to control in the Temperate Zones because winter kills the vector. Last, in some diseases, infected human beings can continue to function more effectively in a cool climate than in the Tropics. This is true of some cases of trichinosis and of amebic dysentery. Yaws, a disease caused by a spirochete, heals by itself when the patient leaves a hot and humid climate for a dry and cool environment.[12]

The pattern of causes of deaths roughly indicates differences between the health situation of industrialized countries in the Temperate Zones and that of the less developed countries in the Tropics. The major differences are that infectious, parasitic, and respiratory diseases account for around 44 percent of the deaths in the developing countries but only 11 percent in the developed countries, while cancer and diseases of the circulatory system together cause 19 percent of the deaths in the developing countries and 47 percent in the developed countries.[13]

Carl M. Stevens points out in a pioneering analysis that the relation between health and economic development may be very complex and that research is badly needed to establish the true relation better. In the short run, improved health is generally thought to result in an increased supply of labor, through increased productivity of the individual, and therefore in increased income. However, much greater benefits of improved health may come rather in the long run and through the improvement of the health of the group or community. Improvement in one individual's health may have little measurable effect on production in agriculture, for example, because the existing organization modes and technology were set up within a framework of existing constraints, including the ill health of most farm laborers. A factory offers an even better example when the pace of the whole production process has been set to adapt to the poor health of the majority of the workers. As Stevens says: "It is reasonable to suppose that . . . ill health exacts its greatest toll on productivity [by] contributing importantly to the failure to adopt otherwise available innovations, both technical and organizational, which have a far greater impact on productivity than that to be had from labor augmentation in the context of the tradi-

12. May, The Ecology of Human Disease, pp. 5, 227.
13. Computed from United Nations, Population Bulletin of the United Nations, no. 7, 1963 (ST/SOA/Ser.N/7), 1965, pp. 111–12.

tional techniques." [14] In the case of agriculture, farmers in poor health have insufficient physical energy both to do their traditional tasks and to invest labor in improved technology; they also lack the mental energy and attention span necessary to plan ahead and in-novate beyond the well-worn grooves of custom. Similar considera-tions apply to nonagricultural pursuits. Sick children do not learn well in school. If students are sick, the resources allocated to educa-tion are partly wasted and schools do not produce individuals with as high a level of basic skills as they would with healthier students. The labor force is also less efficient because people with scarce skills are neither as effectively used nor as productive because of their high incidence of poor health.

As Stevens says, not only does the status of a person's health im-pact on productivity, it is in fact an important part of his welfare. Economic development does not mean only increase in personal in-comes; personal incomes are rather a proxy for individual well-being. While not quantifiable as easily as money incomes, good health may be regarded as an important component of real income.

Among the major diseases influencing mortality patterns and affecting the productivity of people are bilharzia, malaria, river blindness, and a host of other parasitic diseases such as sleeping sickness. The latter was discussed in Chapter 4 in connection with strains of trypanosomiasis that attack animals. The following sec-tions take up the other diseases in turn.

Bilharzia

The debilitating disease bilharzia (schistosomiasis, some-times called snail fever or liver fluke) affects some 150 million to 200 million people in Africa, the Middle East, and Latin America. Millions are afflicted in Mainland China, where the disease is wide-spread in the Yangtze valley and presumably in south China. Ac-cording to doctors in Peking's Anti-Imperialist Hospital, it is China's most serious health problem.[15] In Egypt the countryside is almost

14. "Health, Employment and Income Distribution," World Employment Programme Research Working Paper no. 21, provisional draft (Geneva: Inter-national Labour Organisation, 1975), p. 11.
15. Sally Reston, "Mao's Poem Urges Drive on Virulent Snail Fever," New York Times (July 30, 1971), p. 7. Mao Tse-tung had written of bilharzia's debilitating effects:

saturated with the disease. The World Health Organization, in its Egypt 10 Project, found in six sample villages the incidence among humans was at least 50 percent, and in one village at least 70 percent. Bilharzia is considered by the World Health Organization to be the most important parasitic world health problem. The disease is still out of control and continues to spread to new areas as an unwelcome by-product of dam and canal construction with the migration of infected workers into new areas. (See the map on page 64.)

Bilharzia is a cruel, debilitating, sometimes fatal disease. In its chronic stages, the disease may produce severe, irreversible liver damage, an enlarged spleen, and a bloated abdomen, while the rest of the body becomes emaciated. So far neither a generally applicable cure nor a system of control has been found. There has been some progress in recent years. Understanding of how to cope with the disease has increased. Chemical therapy is being developed. The available cures used to be almost as unpleasant as the disease: a new drug can effectively cure the disease with one injection, but it has side effects and cannot be used in a mass campaign.

There have been a few efforts to establish a cost-benefit analysis of bilharzia control, but the results are somewhat inconclusive. In areas where bilharzia is endemic it is difficult to separate out the economic effects of the disease alone, since the debilitating effects of the disease become associated with malnutrition and confused with the impact of other parasites and other diseases. What is perhaps the best study in the field found that the impact of one variety of the disease, schistosomiasis japonicum, was estimated to cut working ability of patients from 15 to 18 percent in mild cases and 72 to 80 percent in severe cases.[16]

The agent of bilharzia is a parasitic worm, or schistosome, that is a quarter of an inch to an inch in length when fully grown. There are three main species: Schistosoma haematobium, which causes damage chiefly in the bladder and anal regions but often also affects the kidneys and the genital tract in women; S. mansoni, which affects the intestine, spleen, and liver; and S. japonicum, which

---

Green streams, blue hills—but all to what avail?
This tiny germ left even Hua
   To powerlessness;
Weeds choked hundreds of villages, men wasted away;
Thousands of households dwindled, phantoms sang with glee.

16. Tropical Health, p. 236.

1970
U.S.S.R.
AFGHAN-
ISTAN
N.
KOREA
IRAN
1963
S.
KOREA
IRAQ
West Bengal
TAIWAN
Tropic of Cancer
1965-
66
INDIA
YEMEN
ARAB REP.
P.D.R.
OF YEMEN
BANGLA-
DESH
1964
1961
1970-71
1963
1962
ASIA AND THE
WESTERN PACIFIC
Equator
Celebes

GEOGRAPHICAL
DISTRIBUTION OF
BILHARZIA, LEPROSY,
AND CHOLERA

Areas where bilharzia
is prevalent

Areas where 5 or more
in 1,000 of the popula-
tion have leprosy

Outbreaks of cholera
and threatened areas

THE AMERICAS

Tropic of Capricorn

N

Kilometers
0   1000   2000   3000
0   1000   2000
Miles

Tropic of Cancer
MEXICO

GUATEMALA

VENEZUELA
GUYANA
SURINAM
FR.GUIANA
COLOMBIA
Amazon
Equator

AFRICA

BRAZIL

1971
1970
Nile
Tropic
of Cancer

Tocantins
S.Francisco

UP.
VOLTA
Tropic
of
Capricorn

1970-71
CEN.
AFR.REP.
1970-
71
IVORY
COAST
1971
UGANDA
Equator
ZAIRE
KENYA

Tr. of
Capricorn

*The boundaries shown on this map do not
imply endorsement or acceptance by the
World Bank and its affiliates.*

chiefly affects the liver and spleen and which in a child can result in infantilism. The link between the worm and the disease was discovered in 1852 by Theodore Bilharz, but the complicated life cycle of the worm was not fully worked out until 1910.

The life cycle begins with a male and female schistosome mating within a human vein, in which the worm's thorned eggs are laid. The eggs of each female number in the thousands. These eggs work their way into the bladder or intestines, lacerating the host's tissues enroute. They damage the liver and produce a gradual internal poisoning of the victim, then cause hemorrhages in the intestines and interfere with the absorption of food or cause lesions of the bladder that may result in cancer. The eggs are then excreted. The eggs hatch into larval forms that to survive must find a suitable host snail—only certain species are acceptable hosts. Within the snail, the larva goes through a process of development that results in the production of thousands of minute cercariae. These leave the snail and enter the water of the lake, pond, stream, or irrigation ditch and swim about looking for a mammal host. When they find one drinking or bathing in the water, they easily penetrate the skin, reach a vein and travel to the liver or other host organ. Within four to six weeks the cercariae are mature worms; they mate and the cycle begins again.

A human body is sensitive to the invasion of the cercariae and the initial reaction is fever, chills, headaches, or extreme fatigue. The eggs as mentioned above cause substantial damage to the body on their way out. In all forms of bilharzia, there is a weakening of the body and decreased resistance to still other infections.

The disease has been known since antiquity, and in recent years it has become evident that the bilharzia is spreading rapidly in the developing countries and only Japan has succeeded in controling it through strict sanitation measures.

Synthetic organic molluscicides are now available and effective in killing host snails under field conditions in irrigation channels. This also kills fish, however. Snail control in marshes and lakes is more difficult. A control program of killing snails in an area of over 340,000 hectares in Egypt with 750 kilometers of open drains was estimated to cost about $5 million in 1972.

It has been found that most snails in Egypt lose their infections in the winter (January, February, and March). The semitropical countries thus have a considerable advantage in trying to control the disease, although so far this has not yet resulted in successful control of the disease in Egypt.

In the two International Development Association credits for rural development projects in Malawi and the Malagasy Republic extended by the World Bank in 1972, provision was made for bilharzia control. Farmers would be educated in methods of avoiding infection, bilharzia-free water supplies would be provided, and hospital and clinic facilities to cure those infected would be established. Close watch on the results of these projects will be kept to provide information as to how successful these measures turn out to be in both medical and economic terms.

Malaria

Malaria is one of the most important reasons why development in the Tropics has lagged behind. Malaria probably originated in Africa and spread from there to the other Tropics, the sub-Tropics, and parts of the Temperate Zones during the later Roman Empire and the Middle Ages.

The cause of malaria is a protozoan microbe, one of four species of the genus *Plasmodium*. It may spend part of its life cycle in the human body and the rest in one or another of the sixty or seventy species of *Anopheles* mosquito. In the human body the microbes penetrate the liver and the red blood cells, multiplying in the process and destroying the cells. The different species of plasmodia behave somewhat differently in the body. The severest form is *Plasmodium falciparum*, but all can be fatal, all may prostrate the victim through regular recurrence of chills and fever at intervals of one, two, or three days, and all tend, if untreated, to hang on for months and sometimes years.

As winter kills off most of the mosquito vectors of the disease, malaria is more easily controlled in the Temperate Zones. In fact, one of the principal vectors of malaria (and of filariasis), the mosquito *Anopheles gambias*, can only live in the Tropics.[17] The occurrence of malaria is now largely restricted to the Tropics and the poor countries of the world: most of Africa; parts of Central and South America; and west, south and southeast Asia. The World Health Organization has estimated that (outside of Mainland China, northern Vietnam, and North Korea), in 1965, there were around 100

17. John F. Kessel, "The Ecology of Filariasis," in *Studies in Disease Ecology*, ed. Jacques M. May (New York: Hafner, 1961), p. 58.

million cases of malaria in the world from which 1 million people died. This disease has probably had the greatest impact on history and economic development over thousands of years. Malaria's spread contributed to the decline of the Mesopotamian civilizations and of the Roman Empire. It is believed to have killed Alexander the Great and Oliver Cromwell at the height of their careers. It prevented the French from constructing the Panama Canal. Because Africans were more resistant to malaria, it stimulated the introduction and the spread of black slavery into the United States, the Caribbean countries, and Brazil. With yellow fever, it kept European settlers out of most of tropical Africa.

There has been little research on the economic developmental impact of malaria and what there is has not been followed up.[18] In earlier centuries, malaria may have kept people out of areas subject to the disease, but this is no longer the case. Its main impact now is through an increase in number of deaths and a reduction in the efficiency of the labor force.

Children who contract malaria are more severely affected during their childhood—their learning years—than during their adult life—their working years. Still, the effect may be severe in both cases. Adults contracting the disease for the first time are more seriously ill than those who have had it since childhood and survived. Michael Colbourne estimates that it is likely at least one African child in twenty is killed by malaria, and possibly one in ten.[19] Most children affected are seriously sick in spells and their ability to learn is consequently damaged. As the victim gets older, attacks may be less severe but the occasion of an attack may still keep an adult from working. If attacks occur at a time of year when the soil has to be cultivated, the farm weeded, or the crop harvested, they can have a major impact on output. At other times, the disease may not keep the worker from working but it may affect his productivity.

The full economic impact of malaria is difficult to trace. For example, malaria-infected mothers find it difficult or impossible to

18. Among the pioneer works is Robin Barlow's *The Economic Effects of Malaria Eradication* (Ann Arbor: University of Michigan School of Public Health, 1967); see also *American Economic Review* 57 (May 1967), pp. 130–48. Also useful are comments by George H. Borts and Peter Newman, reported with Barlow's AER article, pp. 150–51, 155–57; Michael Colbourne's *Malaria in Africa* (London: Oxford University Press, 1966); and Peter K. Newman's *Malaria Eradication and Population Growth* (Ann Arbor: University of Michigan Bureau of Public Health Economics, 1965).

19. *Malaria in Africa*, p. 34.

breast-feed their children, thus leading to infant malnutrition as well as a lowered resistance to highly prevalent parasitic and viral infections. If infant malnutrition does impact on mental capacity later in life, this would be still another important economic effect of this disease.

The quick eradication of malaria through spraying, as was accomplished in 1947 in Ceylon (now Sri Lanka), may result in an acceleration of population growth—a large number of children continue to be born even though the need to offset losses to malaria is no longer present. It is not clear in such cases whether the economic costs of larger population growth offset the economic benefits from resources unspent in bringing up children who otherwise would have died prematurely from malaria. The gain in welfare and happiness is undeniable, both for those parents whose children survive and for the children who live without being periodically tortured by the disease. Among the other nonquantifiable benefits from eradication is the difference in human creativity and productivity between a person in good health and one who is ill, not to speak of the difference in attitude toward work and in individual initiative.

The nineteenth century saw malaria disappear from northern and most of western Europe and North America. Medicine's introduction of quinine treatment interrupted the transmission of the disease. In the colder temperate climates, frost already eliminated the vector carrying malaria, the mosquito, for part of the year. As many swamps were drained, the mosquito found fewer refuges during that period when it could survive in the temperate climates. Around the end of the nineteenth century, a combination of discoveries resulted in sufficient knowledge about malaria and how it is spread to make possible systematic attempts to roll it back further. After World War II, malaria was essentially eradicated from the American South and the northern shores of the Mediterranean, and brought under control in a few tropical areas such as Sri Lanka, Guyana, and to a large extent India. Malaria is spreading again in Sri Lanka and India. In 1963, only 17 cases were diagnosed in the whole of Sri Lanka, but over 300,000 cases were diagnosed in 1974. The number of cases reported in India climbed to 2.5 million in 1974. In Africa, in light malarious areas such as Rhodesia, Kigezi in Uganda, and some of the forest areas of Liberia and Cameroon, antimalaria insecticide spraying programs have satisfactorily interrupted malaria transmission. In other areas—the north of Cameroon, Tanzania, and the savanna country of west Africa—eradication campaigns were attempted but transmission has continued. So far, an effective and practicable method for stopping the transmission of malaria all over Africa has not been discovered.[20] The map on page 70 depicts areas subject to malaria transmission and areas where eradication of the disease is being consolidated.

In the absence of a completely effective method, there is some doubt whether partial eradication is worth attempting on large tropical land masses. The mosquitoes develop resistance to insecticides.[21] Some species of mosquitoes are even learning how to avoid insecticides. If the disease is only temporarily eradicated and it comes back again, the situation is worse than before: people who lose their partial resistance to the disease may become much more susceptible to severe attacks if they get it again. Since malaria eradication through the use of insecticides and drugs appears to have halted in recent years, the major hope for further progress may be in developing a vaccine against malaria. Some advance has been made in this effort but major problems remain: immunity against one form of malaria may not protect against the others, acquired resistance disappears in time, and it is not known whether a vaccine would merely suppress or could actually destroy the parasite causing malaria. The answer to malaria in most of the Tropics pending any new research successes appears to be combination programs including spraying, draining swamps, clearing of bush, and mass chemotherapy and chemoprophylaxis. Eradication of the disease requires, in other words, a substantial commitment of resources and cooperative effort.

River Blindness

River blindness (onchocerciasis) is a fly-borne infection that, according to World Health Organization estimates, affects approximately 20 million people. Most of those afflicted live in tropical Africa, in the big river valleys, but some are also in Yemen, and limited areas of Mexico, Guatemala, Venezuela, and Colombia. (See the map on pages 72–73.) River blindness causes partial or total loss of sight and fear of the disease keeps people out of considerable areas of fertile land.

The greatest incidence of river blindness is usually in adult males.

20. Ibid., p. 82.
21. The WHO Expert Committee on Malaria reported in 1967 that twenty-four species of the *Anopheles* mosquito had developed resistance to dieldrin or DDT; eleven had resistance to both.

IBRD 12445
October 1976

ASIA AND THE WESTERN PACIFIC

TURKEY
U.S.S.R.
MONGOLIA
N. KOREA
JAPAN
AFGHANISTAN
CHINA
SYRIA
LEB.
ISRAEL
IRAN
S. KOREA
JORDAN
KUWAIT
PAKISTAN
BHUTAN
NEPAL
QATAR
SAUDI ARABIA
UN. ARAB EM.
INDIA
LAO P.D.R.
TAIWAN
Tropic of Cancer
HONG KONG
OMAN
BANGLA-DESH
VIET-NAM
YEMEN ARAB REP.
P.D.R. OF YEMEN
BURMA
THAILAND
PHILIPPINES
KHMER REP.
SRI LANKA
MALAYSIA
Equator
SINGAPORE
INDONESIA
PAPUA NEW GUINEA

AUSTRALIA
Tropic of Capricorn

GEOGRAPHICAL DISTRIBUTION OF MALARIA

Areas subject to malaria transmission

Areas where malaria eradication is being consolidated

Kilometers
0   1000   2000   3000
0   1000   2000
Miles

THE AMERICAS

CUBA
Tropic of Cancer
MEXICO
HAITI
BELIZE
DOMINICAN REP.
JAMAICA
GUATEMALA
NICARAGUA
BARBADOS
EL SALVADOR
HONDURAS
TRINIDAD & TOBAGO
COSTA RICA
VENEZUELA
GUYANA
PANAMA
SURINAM
Canal Zone
COLOMBIA
FR. GUIANA
ECUADOR
Equator

AFRICA

TUNISIA
MOROCCO
FORMER SP. SAHARA
ALGERIA
ARAB REP. OF LIBYA
ARAB REP. OF EGYPT
Tropic of Cancer
PERU
BRAZIL
BOLIVIA
MAURITANIA
MALI
NIGER
SENEGAL
THE GAMBIA
UPPER VOLTA
CHAD
SUDAN
F.T.A.I.
PARAGUAY
Tropic of Capricorn
GUINEA BISSAU
GUINEA
NIGERIA
CEN. AFR. REP.
ETHIOPIA
CHILE
SIERRA LEONE
SOMALIA
LIBERIA
IVORY COAST
GHANA
TOGO
BENIN
CAMEROON
EQ. GUINEA
GABON
CONGO
RWANDA
BURUNDI
UGANDA
KENYA
URUGUAY
ZAIRE
TANZANIA
MALAWI
ARGENTINA
ANGOLA
ZAMBIA
MOZAMBIQUE
RHODESIA
BOTSWANA
MADAGASCAR
Tr. of Capricorn
NAMIBIA
SOUTH AFRICA
SWAZILAND
LESOTHO

The boundaries shown on this map do not imply endorsement or acceptance by the World Bank and its affiliates.

Since river blindness does not shorten life, the blind are not only subtracted from the economically active portion of the community but become a burden to it. Aside from the infection that various species of the Simuliidae fly may carry, their bites are so unpleasant that they make farming or other outdoor activity difficult. (One species of the fly, *Simulium venustrum*, inhabiting Maine, Siberia, and Canada, is known as the "curse of the north" because of the unpleasantness of its bite. But in these latitudes the fly cannot carry the river blindness infection because temperature has been found to be one of the major factors governing the duration of the parasite cycle in the vector.[22]) The complete extent of the tropical area that is affected by the disease-carrying black fly is still unknown. The most heavily infested areas are in parts of the larger African river valleys—the Volta, the Niger, the Congo, and the upper Nile.

Probably the most heavily affected area is the Volta River Basin in Upper Volta and Ghana. The World Health Organization has estimated there may be 100,000 blind from this cause alone in the area. In some villages of Upper Volta and Ghana, practically all male inhabitants are infected. The percentage of blindness reaches 13 to 35 percent and most of the other inhabitants have impaired vision. In many other villages of west and equatorial Africa, more than 50 percent of the inhabitants are infected; typically, 30 percent would have impaired vision and 4 to 10 percent are blind. In such areas, blindness often affects individuals in their twenties and thirties.

In addition to the cost to the community and the individual resulting from total blindness, the various degrees of impairment of vision suffered by others must also have a substantial impact on productivity. In Guatemala, for example, river blindness causes considerable loss of efficiency among workers on the coffee plantations, and there is a steady drain of public health funds to try to keep the disease under control. Another important economic impact of the disease is essentially the depopulation of the alluvial land of the river valleys. People are afraid to live and work on much of what little fertile land is available.

In Upper Volta, for example, the river valleys of the three branches of the Volta are practically deserted, although they are potentially rich for agriculture. The reason is the presence of river blindness. Over half the country's population live on less than one-fourth the country's area, the central plateau, which is on the whole

22. Thomas A. Burch, "The Ecology of Onchocerciasis," in *Studies in Disease Ecology*, p. 74.

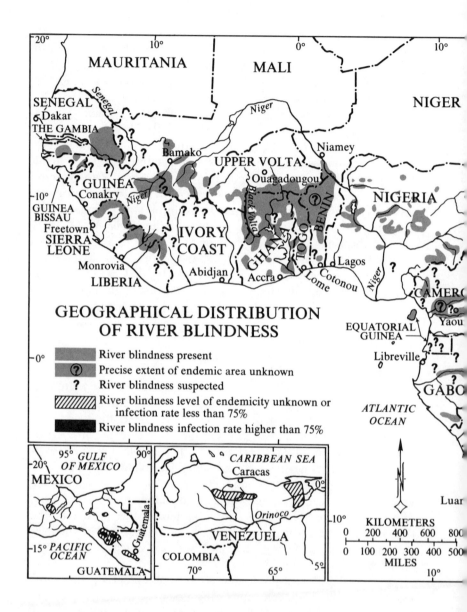

GEOGRAPHICAL DISTRIBUTION
OF RIVER BLINDNESS

River blindness present
Precise extent of endemic area unknown
River blindness suspected
River blindness level of endemicity unknown or infection rate less than 75%
River blindness infection rate higher than 75%

the most poorly endowed with natural resources. With the present techniques of production, land availability for each active person in the central region is insufficient to permit a satisfactory level of food production, considering the disturbing influence of variable weather conditions. Partly in consequence, at least 450,000 to 500,000

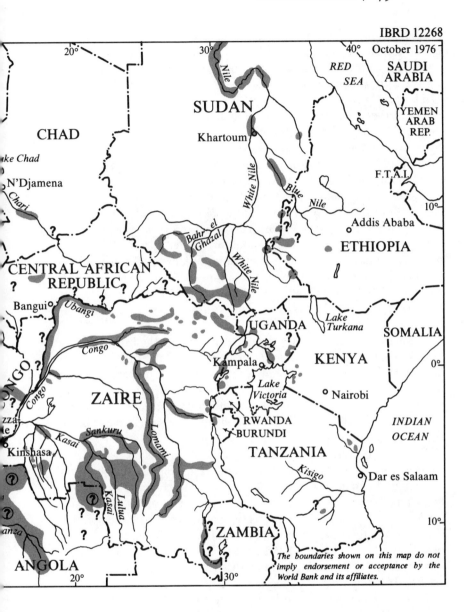

IBRD 12268

Voltaics out of a total population of around 5 million migrate for work to Ghana and the Ivory Coast—around 40 percent of the adult male population. In Uganda, to construct the Owen Falls dam where the Nile flows out of Lake Victoria, it was necessary to eradicate local concentrations of the disease-carrying fly. Fortunately this proved possible. Since then river blindness has been controlled in the area. This had the beneficial by-product of turning a considerable stretch of land in Bugere and the contiguous area of Butembe and Bunya into an important producing area of food and cash crops. Over 75,000 people have resettled there.

Like other parasitic diseases, human infection with river blindness is the result of a complex chain in nature. Although species of fly carry and spread the infinitesimal parasites, they do not produce them. Rather, the nematode, *Onchocerca volvulus*, essentially *causes* river blindness. The adult worms live mainly below the skin, where they may form visible nodules in which one or more worms are coiled. The female worm gives birth to millions of microfilariae during its fifteen year life span. These may move to the skin anywhere in the body and cause lesions or swollen glands. They also may penetrate the eyes where they cause lesions that impair vision or cause blindness. The heaviest infections are in those people who are most heavily loaded with parasites. In forest areas the disease is less severe than in the savanna regions and causes a lower rate of blindness.

Numerous species of black fly actually transmit the infection: the aptly named *Simulium damnosum* in most parts of Africa, *S. neavei* in east and central Africa, and *S. ochraceum*, *S. metallicum* and *S. callidum* in Latin America. The fly bites an infected person, taking up microfilariae that develop into infective larvae in a few days within the fly. These are liberated into the next human being the fly bites, and develop into adult worms.

For its life cycle the fly needs flowing or turbulent water that cools its egg, larva, and pupa stages. Waterfalls, rapids, and spillways providing abundant cool sprays are particularly favorable areas. The flight range of the fly can reach 150 or more kilometers, so its eradication with insecticides is not easy. Small dams constructed for irrigation in arid areas often create favorable breeding sites for these black flies. The spillways of large dams are also favorable, but they can be designed to avoid this and their reservoirs often drown out existing breeding areas.

Much research remains to be done on how to control river blindness. Eradication has been successful in a few confined areas such as the Victoria Nile in Uganda, Kenya, and the Congo River near Kinshasa but the disease was conquered by dosing the rivers with DDT to kill the flyvector in the early stages of its life. In the Murchison Nile in Uganda and Eastern Province in Zaïre) control failed, presumably because the area controlled was not large enough and

the fly reentered the area. No satisfactory methods of mass chemotherapy have yet been found to eradicate the worms and microfilariae
from human beings. In Mexico and Guatemala the nodules contain-
ing the worms are cut out of people, but since all the adult worms
may not be in the nodules, this acts only as a suppressive and not a
complete cure. Aside from the need for more knowledge, a program
of eradication would require much greater resources than most of
the countries affected can handle. A successful program would have
to be able to finance the training of staff, carry out programs of
eradication with sufficient care over the large areas necessary, and
(because of the long life of the worm) continue over a sufficiently
long period of years to eliminate the possibility of reinfection.

Parasitic Worms

A large number of other parasites affect and debilitate
human beings. Often people host two or more parasites at the same
time. Roundworms, pinworms, and whipworms infect over 1 billion people throughout the Tropics and sub-Tropics. (These intestinal helminthiases are respectively the large *Ascaris lumbricoides*, the
Enterobius vermicularis, and the *Trichuris trichiura*.) Hookworm
disease—ancylostomiasis and necatoriasis—infects some 500 million
people in these areas and causes anemia, apathy, and in children
mental and physical retardation. There are about 250 million people
throughout the world who have one or another variety of filariasis
caused by two species of nematodes and spread by the bite of a
mosquito. One of the more unpleasant varieties of this disease is
elephantiasis. About 100 million people suffer this disease in Asia.
Guinea worm, another nematode, affects 50 million to 80 million
people in southeast Asia, India, Africa, and the Middle East.

A World Health Organization report surveyed intestinal worm
infestations among school children in a sample of areas throughout
the world and found high incidence in most cases throughout the
developing countries. Perhaps the highest incidence was in El-
Hadjira, Algeria, where 94 percent had hookworm and 34 percent
had whipworm. In two villages in West Bengal, 75 percent of the
Moslems and 89 percent of the Hindus had hookworm. In a semi-
urban population in Brazil, 25 percent of the population had hookworm, 42 percent another variety of intestinal worm, and 17 percent
and 11 percent still other varieties. The map on page 77 illustrates
the distribution of hookworm disease throughout the world.

Hookworm is characterized by anemia, weakness, fever, and abdominal pain. Heavy infestation may result in mental and physical retardation in children and apathy toward work in adults. Before it was eradicated in the American South, hookworm was probably a main cause for the old stereotype of the Southerner as being lazy, irresponsible, and shiftless. According to one study, labor efficiency in parts of Syria was reduced by as much as 50 percent by heavy hookworm infestation.[23]

Among the most important filaria that are parasitic on humans is Guinea worm (*Filaria medinensis*). In 1947 the number of people having Guinea worm in Asia alone was estimated at over 30 million.[24] It is also widespread in Africa. Although the male is only about one and a half inches long, the female worm reaches a length of over three feet. The female settles in the tissues under the skin. When the worm breaks out, the eggs are scattered in water. These eggs develop in small crustaceans and eventually are taken by a human host in drinking water.

A number of other diseases are significant. Leprosy infects more than 12 million persons, mostly in Africa and south Asia, and most are not under treatment. It has been found recently that the "curative" drug is not as effective as formerly believed. Kala-azar (leishmaniasis or "oriental sore"), dengue ("breakbone fever"), trachoma, and cholera are also significant economic factors from time to time.

Leprosy

Leprosy is now largely restricted to the Tropics. One theory explaining this geographic restriction is that leprosy is related to the many skin abrasions prevalent where insects cause innumerable bites.[25] An estimated 11 million persons are infected in the Tropics, of which almost 4 million are disabled. Only 2 million cases are getting treatment. In 1965 the number of cases was estimated at 6.5 million in Asia, 3.9 million in Africa, 400,000 in the Americas, 50,000 in Europe, and 30,000 in Oceania.[26] Current estimates raise the world total by about 2 million cases. The highest incidences in

23. *Tropical Health*, p. 58.

24. Erwin H. Ackerknecht, *History and Geography of the Most Important Diseases* (New York: Hafner, 1965), p. 134.

25. May, *Ecology of Human Disease*, p. 146.

26. L. M. Bechelli and V. Martínez Domínguez, "The Leprosy Problem in the World," *Bulletin of the World Health Organization* 34 (1966), p. 811.

GEOGRAPHICAL DISTRIBUTION OF HOOKWORM DISEASE

Areas covered by incidence of hookworm disease

ASIA AND THE WESTERN PACIFIC

U.S.S.R. · MONGOLIA · N. KOREA · JAPAN · S. KOREA · CHINA · TURKEY · AFGHANISTAN · LEB. · ISRAEL · IRAN · KUWAIT · PAKISTAN · BHUTAN · NEPAL · JORDAN · QATAR · SAUDI ARABIA · UN. ARAB EM. · OMAN · INDIA · BURMA · LAO P.D.R. · TAIWAN · HONG KONG · BANGLA-DESH · VIET-NAM · YEMEN ARAB REP. · P.D.R. OF YEMEN · THAILAND · PHILIPPINES · SRI LANKA · KHMER REP. · MALAYSIA · SINGAPORE · INDONESIA · PAPUA NEW GUINEA · AUSTRALIA

Tropic of Cancer

Equator

Tropic of Capricorn

THE AMERICAS

Kilometers
0 1000 2000 3000
0 1000 2000
Miles

CUBA · HAITI · DOMINICAN REP. · MEXICO · BELIZE · JAMAICA · GUATEMALA · NICARAGUA · BARBADOS · EL SALVADOR · HONDURAS · COSTA RICA · PANAMA · Canal Zone · TRINIDAD & TOBAGO · VENEZUELA · GUYANA · SURINAM · FR. GUIANA · COLOMBIA · ECUADOR · PERU · BRAZIL · BOLIVIA · PARAGUAY · CHILE · ARGENTINA · URUGUAY

Tropic of Cancer

Equator

Tropic of Capricorn

AFRICA

TUNISIA · MOROCCO · FORMER SP. SAHARA · ALGERIA · ARAB REP. OF LIBYA · ARAB REP. OF EGYPT · MAURITANIA · MALI · NIGER · CHAD · SUDAN · F.T.A.I. · SENEGAL · THE GAMBIA · UPPER VOLTA · GUINEA BISSAU · GUINEA · NIGERIA · CEN. AFR. REP. · ETHIOPIA · SOMALIA · SIERRA LEONE · LIBERIA · IVORY COAST · GHANA · TOGO · BENIN · CAMEROON · EQ. GUINEA · GABON · CONGO · RWANDA · BURUNDI · UGANDA · KENYA · ZAIRE · TANZANIA · MALAWI · ANGOLA · ZAMBIA · MOZAMBIQUE · MADAGASCAR · RHODESIA · BOTSWANA · NAMIBIA · SWAZILAND · LESOTHO · SOUTH AFRICA

Tropic of Cancer

Equator

Tr. of Capricorn

The boundaries shown on this map do not imply endorsement or acceptance by the World Bank and its affiliates.

the world have been found in the Central African Republic (93 for each 1,000 population), Upper Volta (52 for each 1,000), and the Ivory Coast (50 for each 1,000). (See the map on page 64.)

Considerable progress has been made in finding drugs to arrest the progress of the disease and, if used in time, to prevent its disabling and disfiguring aspects. Recently, however, it has been discovered that the standard drug, a sulfone (dapsone or DDS), has limited effectiveness, and some patients develop resistance to it. The main alternative is a phenozine dye compound which discolors the skin. A great deal is still unknown about the disease: whether for example it is only transmitted through long and close association, through direct skin contact, or by breathing germs.

Leishmaniasis

Leishmaniasis is carried by flies and manifests itself either as a debilitating general affliction characterized by enlargement of the spleen, known as Kala-azar, or as a skin disease, known as oriental sore. In Asia, it is endemic in India—Assam, West Bengal, Bihar, Uttar Pradesh and Madras—Bangladesh, some regions in Nepal, and the Middle East. Leishmaniasis is also present in east and north Africa. In Latin America there are only sporadic cases of the disease, but as man penetrates the rain forests a flare-up may occur.[27] Mainland China claims to have eradicated this disease. Leishmaniasis packed Chinese hospital wards and left "hundred of thousands of peasants" dead in the villages and fields, but doctors now say they see only one case in several years.[28]

Yellow Fever and Dengue

The conquest of yellow fever is today one of the few success stories of tropical medicine mostly because it was a major obstacle to the United States' development and expansion at the beginning of this century. Yellow fever, together with malaria, delayed construction of the Panama Canal and made American occupation of Cuba hazardous. (One example of the virulence of the disease be-

27. See the special issue on "Leishmaniasis" of the *Bulletin of the World Health Organization* 44, no. 4 (1971).
28. Reston, "Mao's Poem," p. 7.

fore it was brought under control was the epidemic in Santo Domingo in 1802: it killed 29,000 of the 33,000 veteran soldiers and sailors sent by Napoleon to reconquer the island and garrison New Orleans and the Mississippi valley. This disaster helped induce Napoleon to sell Louisiana to the United States in 1803.) As a result of research by the U.S. Army and Public Health Service, the mosquito vector, Aedes aegypti, was found and, through sanitation measures, was brought under control in the Panama Canal Zone, Cuba, and the southern cities of the United States. An inoculation was later developed by the Rockefeller Foundation against the disease. The mosquito carrying yellow fever stops breeding when temperatures drop below 15°C to 20°C so its range north and south of the equator is determined by these limits. The disease does not now occur in Asia or the southern United States, although the mosquito vector is still present.

This species of mosquito also transmits another disease, dengue, or "breakbone" fever, throughout the tropical and sub-tropical regions including Asia. This disease has only recently been identified. While it is difficult to recognize among other diseases in its endemic phases, it can distinguish itself with epidemics that affect large masses of people in short periods of time. Dengue is not as deadly as yellow fever and the disease only lasts three or four days as it sweeps through a community. Climate particularly affects dengue: the viruses causing the disease are transmitted by the bite of the aegypti mosquito only when the temperature is above 20°C to 22°C, while another vector of the disease, the mosquito Aedes scutellaris, is restricted geographically to a narrow band of the Tropics.[29]

Cholera

Cholera is a bacteria disease transmitted through contaminated food. It can spread anywhere in the world, but its base is in the deltas of the Ganges and Brahmaputra rivers in south Asia and the island of Celebes in Indonesia, where it is endemic. Cholera is no longer a serious public health problem in countries with adequate medical facilities, that is, in more developed countries. With anti-

29. See Charles L. Wisseman and Benjamin H. Sweet, "The Ecology of Dengue," in Studies in Disease Ecology, pp. 15–44.

biotics and replenishment of body fluids, recovery is almost always swift, leaving no after effects. In the 1961–71 pandemic (see the map on page 64), cases appeared in many parts of Asia, Africa, and a few cities of Europe. In 1971 there may have been more than 20,000 deaths from the disease. One of the main economic consequences of cholera was that, to protect themselves, many less developed countries with inadequate medical facilities in some cases cut off trade with countries in which cholera appeared.

8. Health Research

In a true sense it may be said that tropical medicine is
the midwife of economic progress in the underdeveloped
areas of the world.

STACY MAY

The Tropics are more hospitable to most human diseases
than the temperate climates. The Tropics favor the multiplication of
parasite species, the causes of diseases, and their insect vectors. Because of the absence of winter, the assault on humans is more continuous. Some diseases formerly present in temperate climates are
now endemic only to the Tropics, where they are harder to stamp
out. Some diseases that are still present in both the Tropics and the
Temperate Zones are harder to handle in the Tropics. For example,
bacillary dysentery can occur almost anywhere. Spread of the disease
usually depends on the house fly population; in turn, the speed with
which the fly multiplies depends on temperature. At 16°C it takes
forty-four days for the fly to develop from egg to adult. The time
decreases to sixteen days at 25°C and ten days at 30°C.[1]

Medicine and the Tropics

The diseases that have been mentioned, it should be noted,
are the diseases that are primarily restricted to the Tropics. But, in
addition, the less developed countries also have the full set of diseases still prevalent in the Temperate Zones, among which tuber-
culosis is probably the most important. To combat Temperate
Zone diseases, developing countries are able to take over medical
technology from the more developed countries. For diseases prevalent

1. May, *Ecology of Human Disease*, p. 165.

mainly in the Tropics, in most cases, no known effective cures or economically feasible prevention measures as yet exist.

It is highly likely that insufficient resources are being devoted to research for answers to the tropical diseases—this could be reasonably inferred from the lack of attention paid to the problem by development economists and development planners.[2]

Developing countries spend comparatively little on research—current curative and preventative needs are so overpowering. Of the $300 million spent annually by international agencies and bilateral donors for health projects in less developed countries, it is doubtful if more than $30 million is spent on research. One country, the United States, spends ten times this amount on cancer research alone; annual expenditures on cancer research in all of the developed countries are around $1 billion a year. It was only in 1975 that the World Health Organization hoped to establish a research center in Africa to work on tropical diseases and to encourage the formation of a network of institutes, clinics, and field hospitals working on tropical diseases.

One of the reasons for the neglect of the impact of disease is the natural carrying-over to the less developed countries of the usual unformulated assumptions with which economists from the developed countries operate. That is, it is assumed that most people are healthy and that ill health is not a major economic constraint. Further, most economists visiting or working in tropical countries do so at a level of comfort and health protection that is not available to the mass of peoples in the Tropics. Similar high levels of health protection are generally at the command of the tiny governmental and economic elite in the developing countries themselves, and local development economists and planners form a part of this elite.[3]

2. In *Tropical Health* the National Academy of Sciences commented:

The staff and Advisory Committee concerned with the present survey were not unaware of the fact that tremendous progress in tropical health could be achieved by the mere application of knowledge already in existence— if only poverty and lack of education were not in the way. It was also realized, however, that in almost all the important diseases of the tropics . . . there were also gross deficiencies in our knowledge which called for systematic research or development or both (p. viii).

3. When the industrialized countries were in the early stages of development, towns were unhealthier than the countryside; in the developing world today the situation is the reverse. The UN estimated the crude death rate for 1960 in rural areas of less developed countries as 21.7 per 1,000 and only 15.4 for urban areas. See *Demographic Trends in the World and the Major Regions, 1950–1970* (E/Conf.60/BP/1), Table 12.

Economists are not guilty alone of this insensitivity to the real health position—most medical schools, teachers, and doctors in the developing countries are also part of this privileged elite.[4] As a part of the "technological demonstration effect," these doctors are usually preoccupied with the medical problems that are the concern of the medical school teachers and doctors in the more developed countries. That is to say, they worry about degenerative diseases such as cancer and heart disease rather than the infectious, parasitic diseases from which the majority of the population suffer. And, in fact, the doctors in the developing countries often are mainly concerned with these diseases because these are the diseases of their patients, the tiny, economically privileged elite. In a typical developing country the bulk of the doctors practice in the capital city: this is true for example of 54 percent of the doctors in Kenya, 74 percent in Colombia, and 82 percent in Guatemala.[5]

In 1881, Vicomte Ferdinand Marie de Lesseps, the promoter of the Suez Canal, failed in the attempt to build a canal across the Isthmus of Panama, defeated by malaria and yellow fever. In the 1904–14 period, the U.S. Army engineers succeeded in building the canal because research had found the cause and the vector of the diseases. The United States began the construction by first undertaking an expensive and widespread program of sanitation to eradicate the disease-carrying mosquitoes. The prerequisite for success was, in other words, preliminary investment in public health. Since then, most large construction projects in the Tropics have been careful to take steps to protect their workers against the local diseases, but such measures are not taken for the bulk of the economy and the vast majority of the population.

During World War II there were several occasions when there was something like a controlled experiment of how people from developed countries, with their background of good health and good nutrition, would make out in the Tropics when most of the normal comforts and protections were removed. In Guadalcanal, supply conditions were such that neither the American nor Japanese military could provide normal levels of protection against tropical disease. Soldiers from the more developed countries were forced to live

---

4. See Michael J. Sharpston, "Health and Development" [a review of *Doctor Migration and World Health* and *Auxiliaries in Health Care*], *The Journal of Development Studies* 9 (April 1973), pp. 455–60.

5. World Bank, "Background Paper on Health," restricted circulation memorandum of the Development Economics Department (Washington, D.C., October 1974), p. 88.

almost on a par with natives in this respect. The official U.S. Army history comments that malaria proved the greatest single factor reducing the effectiveness of South Pacific troops, causing five times more casualties than enemy action.[6] The First Marine Division in action on Guadalcanal between August 7 and December 10, 1942, had 10,635 casualties: 1,472 resulted from gunshot wounds, but 5,749 malaria cases had put men out of action. In November alone malaria put 3,283 into the hospital. The Japanese medical history of the war estimated that two-thirds of all Japanese deaths were caused by illness—malaria, beri-beri, and dysentery. Major General Tadashi Sumiyoshi, commander of the 17th Army Artillery, stated that throughout the October 1942 counteroffensive he had been so weakened by malaria that he had found it difficult to make decisions.[7]

When the present industrialized countries were still poor, there was greater recognition of the importance of disease as a factor in economic development. Public health measures were in the very beginning based on a recognition of the fundamental problem, the relation between disease and poverty. The report of Sir Edwin Chadwick in 1850, *The Sanitary Condition of the Labouring Population of Great Britain*, which initiated the modern public health movement, was based on the premise that "poverty and disease formed a vicious circle" and that action had to be taken against disease if progress were to be made against poverty.[8]

Essentially, the first substantial progress in health in the industrialized countries in the last century came through purification of water supplies and sanitary disposition of fecal waste. Then, further progress was made through the various research discoveries of the germ causes of disease and control of the insect vectors.[9]

In today's developing countries, the sheer obtrusiveness of disease has led governments to try to do something about it. But because economists have refused to recognize the significance of the prevalent

6. John Miller, Jr., *Guadalcanal: The First Offensive* (Washington, D.C.: Department of the Army Historical Division, 1949), p. 225.

7. Ibid., pp. 159, 209, and 229n. It is significant that the only worldwide useful atlases of diseases that exist are one prepared for the American armed forces and one that was being prepared for the German armed forces in World War II.

8. Charles E. A. Winslow, *The Cost of Sickness and the Price of Health* (Geneva: World Health Organization, 1951), p. 9.

9. Ibid., p. 18.

diseases for development, little attention has been paid to economic factors in allocating resources to disease control compared with other uses or in securing maximum economic benefit from what resources were made available. It is possible that the decisions that were taken have been optimal but it is highly improbable. The fact that much of the medical attention in developing countries has been concentrated on curative medicine for the small elite rather than preventive medicine for the vast majority does not argue that development objectives were being efficiently pursued.[10]

Development Finance and Health

International assistance in health began over a century ago in efforts to control the spread of communicable diseases across frontiers. The International Sanitary Bureau, parent of the Pan American Health Organization, was founded in 1902. The Rockefeller Foundation started its activities in 1913 with heavy emphasis on endemic disease control. After World War II the World Health Organization was founded. In recent years, following family planning experience, many donor countries have put a growing emphasis on low-cost health delivery systems that can reach the poor. Family planning and health activities are so interwoven that it is difficult to distinguish between aid expenditures on population and aid expenditures on health.

The bulk of external aid has gone to training and technical assistance rather than to the financing of research on the special problems of the developing countries or on capital costs. In 1972 the World Health Organization, Pan American Health Organization, and UNICEF together spent $175 million, the bulk of this in developing countries. The United States and the Federal Republic of Germany each spent about $42 million, and all the other bilateral donors together spent about the same amount for a world total of about $300 million in international assistance to the health sector of less developed countries.

Most of the assistance covered in these figures was probably devoted to trying to improve the health conditions in the developing countries, considering health as a consumer good, as an important

10. Typically, of the health budget in a less developed country, two-thirds to three-quarters of expenditures are allocated to curative care, according to "Background Paper on Health," p. 75.

part of the standard of living. At the same time, expenditures on eradication or control of disease have an impact on economic productivity, and one of the most important developments in recent years has been the way in which such expenditures have been creeping into various project investments as it has become evident to the project analysts that disease control was essential to the success of the projects. Practice has outrun theory, as has been often true in development economics.

The World Bank began to make loans for drinking water and sewerage projects in 1961. In 1970, the Bank worked out a cooperative arrangement with the World Health Organization under which the latter would help find and prepare drinking water, sewerage, and storm drainage projects for the Bank. By 1974 the total of World Bank loans and IDA credits for water supply and sewerage had surpassed $1,500 million, and the annual level of new lending was running about $300 million to $500 million a year.

Action to improve drinking water and sanitation is undoubtedly one of the most effective ways in which to begin to improve health in the developing countries just as it was in the industrialized countries. In fact, the UN Advisory Committee on the Application of Science and Technology to Development recommended that "primarily greater attention should be given to the provision of communal water supplies of high quality. . . . In developing countries the absence or imperfection of the water supply are contributory causes to the ravages of cholera, enteric fevers, bacillary and amebic dysentery, and the all-pervading diarrhoeal diseases. It is estimated that these diseases affect no less than 500 million people each year . . ." [11] This conclusion seems fairly safe to advance, but the lack of appreciation by economists of the importance of health to development has meant that little basic research has been done to measure more precisely how much of a contribution safe water, for example, might make. As Jeremy Warford has pointed out, everyone acknowledges the health benefits of piped water supply, but there is no firm statistical evidence to demonstrate what will happen in a town or region when water is made available. "[N]ot only are we unaware of the effects of improved water supply on health in monetary terms," Warford writes, "we do not even know what the *physical*

11. United Nations, Economic and Social Council, Advisory Committee on the Application of Science and Technology to Development, *World Plan of Action for the Application of Science and Technology to Development*, rev. ed. (E/4962/rev.1/ST/ECA/146), 1971, p. 222.

benefits are." [12] It was not until 1975 that an international interagency program began to focus on potable water supply and sewage disposal. The International Development Research Centre of Canada, UNICEF, the UN Environment Program, the World Health Organization, and the World Bank have now started joint action to strengthen international, regional, and national research programs, help provide training and technical services in this field, and expand help to rural community water supplies.

The importance of taking action to improve health conditions an integral part of a project has become more and more evident to project analysts in many sectors. This approach dominated population planning when the World Bank began lending for this purpose in 1970. Of the total project costs of $230 million in the Bank's population projects, almost 60 percent is for health facilities for mother and child care. The Bank's first urban population project, financing a sites and services scheme in Dakar, included five health centers at a total cost of $400,000. Similar provision is likely in future projects. In the agricultural sector, health components are increasingly included.

In some land settlement schemes, health facilities have been provided as part of the "minimum package" necessary to make the settlement viable. For instance, in planning Colombia's Caqueta land colonization project in 1971, health services were from the outset considered an important factor influencing settlers' decisions to reside permanently in a remote area with high prevalence of disease. In other settlement schemes, health was a social service to be provided at an increasingly sophisticated level as the settlement became established and financial resources permitted—some examples include the 1972 Alto Turi land settlement project in Brazil and Malaysia's Jengka Triangle project in 1970 and 1973. Project justification in these cases stresses the need for the facilities if settlers are to remain in the area rather than the importance of improving health levels. A few rural development schemes have also had health components, either to guard against health menaces accompanying the project—for example, schistosomiasis control with the irrigation aspects of a rural development project in Karonga, Malawi, during 1971—or as part of an attempt at integrated social and economic development—for example, the rural development project in Mauritius during 1973.

12. "The Role of Economics in Municipal Water Supply: Theory and Practice," restricted circulation memorandum of the Public Utilities Department, World Bank (Washington, D.C., December 1971), p. 1.

Sometimes the trend has been to add health components after the first phase of a project—some examples are Malawi's Shire valley agricultural development project in 1968 and the Lilongwe agricultural development project in 1968, 1971, and the present. The latter project did not include a health component in its previous phases, but the subsequent construction of health centers generated the most active self-help effort among the rural people as some thirty-five health posts were constructed. One example of a development project that also included provisions for water supply, with the hope that this would benefit health, was the rural development fund project of Upper Volta in 1972. Finally, in some cases, human health could benefit as a side effect of a project; trypanosomiasis affects both cattle and humans, and the successful eradication of the tsetse under the 1973 agricultural development project in Rwanda will certainly be a benefit to human as well as animal health.[13]

Environmental health measures against specific diseases have been a common element in projects—for example, mollusciciding in Karonga against schistosomiasis, dispensing malaria prophylactics and helminthicides in the Caqueta project, and spraying houses against malaria in the Alto Turi project. A second phase of the Caqueta project may have nutrition and health education components; already there are rural health promoters, selected from settlers' families and trained locally, who perform first aid, give vaccinations, provide aid at childbirth, disperse malaria and helminthiasis drugs, and distribute birth control materials.

Some of the World Bank's education sector projects have also had a health impact. A project in Greece in 1970 financed health manpower training, mainly for hospital staff. An education project in Uganda in 1971 supported the training of paramedical personnel for rural preventive services. Another education project in Tanzania in 1973 provided for the training of doctors who will supervise the health care given by paramedical personnel in the rural areas. A 1973 education project in Zambia included, in addition to paramedical training, a Health Services Training School at Ndola built around a new 650-bed hospital to train hospital staff.

The UN Development Programme (UNDP) has also become more and more conscious of the importance of health to development. UNDP has financed research on bilharzia, helped governments to eradicate treponematosis (a disease found in some west African countries and characterized by lesions of the skin, cartilage, and bone), and supported action against leprosy and river blindness.

In 1972 the international aid community embarked on an experiment of coordinated action against a single disease, river blindness, as a necessary means to help the economic development of a number of west African countries. The threat of river blindness prevents large populations from exploiting small areas of fertile soil available to them. It is such an evident obstacle to economic development that it makes obvious sense for international investment agencies to join with the health organizations to take action against it. Consequently, a steering committee composed of representatives of UNDP, the World Health Organization, the Food and Agriculture Organization, and the World Bank was set up in 1972. The steering committee prepares and coordinates a $120 million, twenty-year (1974–94) action program against the disease. The World Bank, on behalf of the steering committee and the African governments concerned, has organized a consultative group of interested governments and international agencies to mobilize finances for the program. If this program proves successful, it will not only have a substantial economic impact on west Africa but will also provide a model for the international community's assault on other major diseases that hold back developing countries.

At the beginning of 1975 it seemed fair to conclude that governments and international development agencies had agreed that action against disease in the less developed countries is as an important component of any program to help economic development. A number of experiments were initiated. What has been done so far is a promising beginning, but only a beginning. Practically nothing has been done in the way of systematic economic analysis of the various specific obstacles to economic development posed by disease and of the economic and social costs and benefits of projects to remove them. Without this basic information it is impossible for a government or aid agency to allocate investment optimally between disease control as such and other more conventional investment projects. In the meantime, it is highly improbable that the existing distribution of resources is anywhere near optimal.

9. Conclusions

Man is embedded in nature. The biological sciences of
recent years has been making this a more urgent fact of
life. The new, hard problem will be to cope with the dawn-
ing, intensifying realization of just how interlocked we
are.

LEWIS THOMAS

This book has explored special constraints affecting economic development in the Tropics that are additional to those now
faced by countries in the Temperate Zones. Whether in a particular
case the tropical constraints are the ruling ones at the moment does
not matter in this analysis. Sooner or later they will become important as other constraints are removed or disappear. While the
peculiarly tropical problems identified in this book are probably
among the most important, I have indicated there may well be other
important tropical problems. Whether this makes the development
threshold higher for tropical countries than that faced by the Temperate Zone countries that first began modern economic growth
again is not an important question today. What matters today is
whether there is a special group of countries that have a set of constraints on their development that cannot be handled by an easy
transfer or adaptation of existing technology from the developed
Temperate Zone countries. One theme of this book is that there is
such a group and it comprises the countries in the Tropics.

The second theme of the book is that special measures, particularly in research, have to be taken to find ways of overcoming the
special obstacles posed by the Tropics. In recent years the international development community has made a promising beginning in
this. It is quite possible that when eventually the tropical constraints
are mastered, the same characteristics that now hinder the Tropics
may then give them advantages over the Temperate Zones. This may
especially prove true in agriculture. As pests, predators, and diseases

are controlled and the application of water to crops is regulated, the heat, sunlight, the almost infinite variety of tropical life, and the more rapid evolution characteristics of the Tropics should make tropical agriculture more productive than that of the Temperate Zones. In livestock, there is already beginning to exist a sufficient stock of knowledge to make this forecast credible. In the last thirty years, rapid economic growth came to the sub-Tropics; in the next fifty years, with a sufficient concentration of international effort on solving the peculiar problems of the Tropics, economic growth could truly take off.

Bibliography

Abel-Smith, B. "Health Priorities in Developing Countries: The Economist's Contribution." *International Journal of Health Services* 2 (February 1972):5–12.

Ackerknecht, Erwin H. *History and Geography of the Most Important Diseases.* New York: Hafner, 1965.

Ahn, Peter M. *West African Soils.* West African Agriculture, edited by Frederick R. Irvine, vol. 1, 3d ed. London: Oxford University Press, 1970.

Arakawa, H., ed. *Climates of Southern and Western Asia.* World Survey of Climatology, edited by Helmut E. Landsberg, vol. 9. Amsterdam: Elsevier, 1972.

Aubert de la Rüe, Edgar; François Bourlière; and Jean-Paul Harroy. *The Tropics.* New York: Knopf, 1957.

Barlow, Robin. *The Economic Effects of Malaria Eradication.* Ann Arbor: University of Michigan, School of Public Health, 1968.

Basta, Samir S., and Anthony Churchill. "Iron Deficiency Anemia and the Productivity of Adult Males in Indonesia." Staff Working Paper no. 175. Washington, D.C.: World Bank, April 1974.

Bauer, Pèter Tamàs. *Dissent on Development: Studies and Debates in Developing Economics.* Cambridge, Mass.: Harvard University Press, 1972.

Bechelli, L. M., and V. Martínez Domínguez. "The Leprosy Problem in the World." *Bulletin of the World Health Organization* 34 (1966): 811–26.

Berg, Alan D. "Malnutrition and National Development." *Foreign Affairs* 46 (October 1967):126–36.

Bleier, Michael E. "African Trypanosomiasis." Mimeographed. Washington, D.C.: Johns Hopkins University School for Advanced International Studies, 1968.

Borts, George H. "Discussion" on "The Economic Effects of Malaria Eradication." *American Economic Review* 57 (May 1967):149–51.

Boulding, Kenneth E. "Is Economics Culture-Bound?" *American Economic Review* 60 (May 1970):406–11.

Bulletin of the World Health Organization. Special issue on "Leishmaniasis." Vol. 44, no. 4 (1971).

Buxton, Patrick A. *The Natural History of Tsetse Flies: An Account of the Biology of the Genus* Glossina *(Diptera).* London: Lewis, 1955.

Cairns, Robert. "Sunny Corsica, French Morsel in the Mediterranean." *National Geographic* 144 (September 1973):400–23.

Chang, Jen-Hu. "The Agricultural Potential of the Humid Tropics." *The Geographical Review* 63 (July 1968):333–61.

Chaudhry, Mahinder D. "Economic Distance among Regions: A Statistical Analysis." *Economic Development and Cultural Change* 19 (July 1971):527–44.

Chenery, Hollis B. "Land: The Effect of Resources on Economic Growth." In *Economic Development with Special Reference to East Asia,* edited by Kenneth Berrill, pp. 19–49. New York: St. Martin's 1964.

————, and Lance Taylor. "Development Patterns: Among Countries and Over Time." *The Review of Economics and Statistics* 50 (November 1968):391–416.

Ciba Research Laboratories, "Bilharziasis and its Treatment with Ambilhar." Basel, 1967.

Colbourne, Michael. *Malaria in Africa.* London: Oxford University Press, 1966.

Collis, W. R. F.; I. Dema; and A. Omololu. "On the Ecology of Child Nutrition and Health in Nigerian Villages: II. Dietary and Medical Surveys." *Tropical and Geographical Medicine* 14 (September 1962): 201–29.

Davey, T. H., and W. P. H. Lightbody. *The Control of Diseases in the Tropics: A Handbook for Medical Practitioners.* London: Lewis, 1956.

Demuth, Richard H. "The International Agricultural Research Consultative Group." *International Development Review* 13 ([September] 1971):45–46.

Diuguid, Lewis H. "Northeast Still Challenges Brazil." *Washington Post* (July 1, 1971):F1, F3.

Ellis, Howard S., and Henry C. Wallich, eds. *Economic Development for Latin America.* New York: St. Martin's, 1961.

Enke, Stephen. "Economists and Development: Rediscovering Old Truths." *Journal of Economic Literature* 7 (December 1969): 1125–39.

Erickson, R. L. "Summary Proposals for Investigations of Techniques in Mineral Exploration Suited to the Special Needs of Tropical Regions." Memorandum of the Geological Survey, U.S. Interior Department, Washington, D.C., January 1974.

Feldstein, Martin S. "Health Sector Planning in Developing Countries." *Economica* 37 (May 1970):139–63.

Fisher, Charles A. *South-east Asia: A Social, Economic, and Political Geography.* 2nd ed. New York: Dutton, 1966.

Frankel, S. Herbert. "Economic Changes in Africa in Historical Perspective." In *Economic Development in the Long Run,* edited by Alexander J. Youngson, pp. 211–28. London: Allen and Unwin, 1972.

Fransen, J. M.; J. C. Gerring; C. P. McMeekan; and D. Stoops. "World Bank Lending for Livestock Development." Restricted circulation memorandum of the Agriculture and Rural Development Department, World Bank. Washington, D.C., October 1971.

Furtado, Celso. "The Development of Brazil." *Scientific American* 209 (September 1963):208–20.

——. *Obstacles to Development in Latin America.* Translated by Charles Ekker. Garden City, N.Y.: Anchor, 1970.

Gaitskell, Arthur. *Gezira: A Story of Development in the Sudan.* London: Faber and Faber, 1959.

Galbraith, John Kenneth. "Conditions for Economic Change in Underdeveloped Countries." *Journal of Farm Economics* 33 (November 1951):689–96.

Georgescu-Roegen, Nicholas. "The Economics of Production." *American Economic Review* 60 (May 1970):1–9.

——. *The Entropy Law and the Economic Process.* Cambridge, Mass.: Harvard University Press, 1971.

Godfrey, D. G.; R. Killick-Kendrick; and W. Furguson. "Bovine Trypanosomiasis in Nigeria: Observations on Cattle Trekked along a Trade Cattle Route through Areas Infested with Tsetse Fly." *Annals of Tropical Medicine and Parasitology* 59 (September 1965): 255–69.

Gorou, Pierre. *Les Pays Tropicaux: Principes d'une Géographie Humaine et Economique,* 5th ed. Paris: Presses Universitaires de France, 1969.

Griffiths, J. F., ed. *Climates of Africa.* World Survey of Climatology, edited by Helmut E. Landsberg, vol. 10. Amsterdam: Elsevier, 1972.

Grigg, David B. *The Harsh Lands: A Study in Agricultural Development.* New York: St. Martin's, 1970.

Hadlow, Leonard. *Climate, Vegetation & Man.* New York: Philosophical Library, 1953.

Hahn, F. H. "Some Adjustment Problems." *Econometrica* 38 (January 1970):1–17.

Hance, William A. *The Geography of Modern Africa.* New York: Columbia University Press, 1964.

Haskell, Peter T. "Locust Control: Ecological Problems and International Pests." In *The Careless Technology: Ecology and Inter-*

national Development, edited by M. Taghi Farvar and John P. Milton, pp. 499–526. Garden City, N.Y.: Doubleday [Natural History], 1972.

Higgins, Benjamin H. *Economic Development: Principles, Problems, and Policies.* Rev. ed. New York: Norton, 1968.

Hirschman, Albert O. *Journeys Toward Progress: Studies of Economic Policymaking in Latin America.* New York: Twentieth Century Fund, 1963.

―――, ed. *Latin American Issues: Essays and Comments.* New York: Twentieth Century Fund, 1961.

Hoagland, Jim. "Africa: Fragments in the Mind." *Washington Post* (February 18, 1973):B1.

Hodder, Bramwell W. *Economic Development in the Tropics.* London: Methuen, 1968.

Hughes, Charles C., and John M. Hunter. "The Role of Technological Development in Promoting Disease in Africa." In *The Careless Technology: Ecology and International Development,* edited by M. Taghi Farvar and John P. Milton, pp. 69–101. Garden City, N.Y.: Doubleday [Natural History], 1972.

Huntington, Ellsworth. *Civilization and Climate.* New Haven: Yale University Press, 1915.

Isbister, Claude M. "Comments on 'Sector Program Paper—The Non Fuel Mineral Industry'." Memorandum of the Executive Directors, World Bank. Washington, D.C., January 1974.

Jahnke, Hans E. *The Economics of Controlling Tsetse Flies and Cattle Trypanosomiasis in Africa Examined for the Case of Uganda.* Munich: IFO–Institut für Wirtschaftforschung, 1974.

James, Preston E. *Introduction to Latin America: The Geographic Background of Economic and Political Problems.* New York: Odyssey, 1964.

―――, and Hibberd V. B. Kline, Jr. *A Geography of Man.* Waltham, Mass.: Blaisdell, 1966.

Joint FAO/WHO Expert Committee on African Trypanosomiasis. *African Trypanosomiasis.* Technical Report Series no. 434. Geneva: World Health Organization, 1969.

Jones, William Henry Samuel, and G. G. Ellett. *Malaria: A Neglected Factor in the History of Greece and Rome.* Cambridge: Macmillan and Bowes, 1907.

Jones, William O. "Environment, Technical Knowledge, and Economic Development in Tropical Africa." *Food Research Institute Studies* 5 (1965):101–16.

Kamarck, Andrew M. " 'Capital' and 'Investment' in Developing Countries." *Finance & Development* 8 (June 1971):2–9.

————. *The Economics of African Development*. Rev. ed. New York: Praeger, 1971.

————. "Review of *Disease and Economic Development* . . . by Burton A. Weisbrod [and others]." *Journal of Economic Literature* 13 (March 1975): 107–09.

Kellogg, Charles E. "We Seek; We Learn." In *Soil, The Yearbook of Agriculture*. U.S. Department of Agriculture, pp. 1–11. Washington, D.C.: Government Printing Office, 1957.

Kendrew, Wilfrid G. *The Climates of the Continents*. 5th ed. Oxford: Clarendon, 1961.

Kindleberger, Charles P. *Economic Development*. 2nd ed. New York: McGraw-Hill, 1965.

King, Maurice H. *Medical Care in Developing Countries: A Primer on the Medicine of Poverty and a Symposium from Makere*. Nairobi: Oxford University Press, 1967.

King, Timothy, and others. *Population Policies and Economic Development: A World Bank Staff Report*. Baltimore: Johns Hopkins University Press, 1974.

Klarman, Herbert E. *The Economics of Health*. New York: Columbia University Press, 1965.

————. "Present Status of Cost-Benefit Analysis in the Health Field." *American Journal of Public Health* 57 (November 1967):1948–53.

Kumar, Ladapuram S. S., and others. *Agriculture in India*. 3 vols. Bombay: Asia Publishing House, 1963.

Lambert, L. Don. "The Role of Climate in the Economic Development of Nations." *Land Economics* 47 (November 1971):339–44.

Langridge, W. P.; R. J. Kernaghan; and P. E. Glover. "A Review of Recent Knowledge of the Ecology of the Main Vectors of Trypanosomiasis." *Bulletin of the World Health Organization* 28 (1963): 671–701.

Laurie, William. "Survey before Service: Observations on Relations between Agriculture, Parasite Load, and Nutrition on a Tropical African Island." *The Lancet* 2 (October 16, 1954):801–2.

Lee, Douglas H. K. *Climate and Economic Development in the Tropics*. New York: Harper, 1957.

Leibenstein, Harvey. *Economic Backwardness and Economic Growth: Studies in the Theory of Economic Development*. New York: Wiley, 1957.

Leurquin, Philippe. "Cotton Growing in Colombia: Achievements and Uncertainties." *Food Research Institute Studies* 6 (1966):143–80.

Lewis, William Arthur. *The Theory of Economic Growth*. Homewood, Ill.: Irwin, 1955.

Lipton, Michael. "Population, Land and Decreasing Returns to Agriculture Labour." *Bulletin of the Oxford University Institute of Economics and Statistics* 26 (May 1964):123–57.

MacLeish, Kenneth. "The Top End of Down Under." *National Geographic* 143 (February 1973):145–74.

McMullen, Donald B. "Schistosomiasis Control in Theory and Practice." *American Journal of Tropical Medicine and Hygiene* 12 (May 1963): 288–95.

Martin, Edwin M. "Development Co-operation: Efforts and Policies of the Members of the Development Assistance Committee." 1972 review. Paris: Organisation for Economic Co-operation and Development, Development Assistance Committee, 1972.

Masefield, G. B. "Agricultural Changes in Uganda: 1945–1960." *Food Research Institute Studies* 3 (May 1962):87–124.

May, Jacques M. *The Ecology of Human Disease*. New York: MD Publications, 1958.

———, ed. *Studies in Disease Ecology*. New York: Hafner, 1961.

Meier, Gerald M. *Leading Issues in Economic Development: Studies in International Poverty*. 2nd ed. New York: Oxford University Press, 1970.

Mellor, John W. *The Economics of Agricultural Development*. Ithaca: Cornell University Press, 1966.

Miller, John, Jr. *Guadalcanal: The First Offensive*. United States Army in World War II, the War in the Pacific. Washington, D.C.: Department of the Army, Historical Division, 1949.

Miracle, Marvin P. *Agriculture in the Congo Basin: Tradition and Change in African Rural Economies*. Madison: University of Wisconsin Press, 1967.

Mushkin, Selma. "Health Programming in Developing Nations." *International Development Review* 6 (March 1964):7–12.

Myrdal, Gunnar. *Asian Drama: An Inquiry into the Poverty of Nations*. New York: Twentieth Century Fund, 1968.

National Academy of Sciences–National Research Council, Division of Medical Sciences. *Tropical Health: A Report on a Study of Needs and Resources*. Washington, D.C., 1962.

Nelson, Michael. *The Development of Tropical Lands: Policy Issues in Latin America*. Baltimore: Johns Hopkins University Press, 1973.

Newman, Peter. "Discussion" on "The Economic Effects of Malaria Eradication." *American Economic Review* 57 (May 1967):155–57.

———. *Malaria Eradication and Population Growth, with Special Reference to Ceylon and British Guiana*. Ann Arbor: University of Michigan, School of Public Health, 1965.

Nisbet, Charles T., ed. *Latin America: Problems in Economic Development.* New York: Free Press, 1969.

Osmundsen, John A. "Science: Battle Is On Against a Dread Crippler." *New York Times* (August 22, 1965):8E.

Paddock, William, and Elizabeth Paddock. *We Don't Know How: An Independent Audit of What They Call Success in Foreign Assistance.* Ames: Iowa State University Press, 1973.

Pan American Health Organization, Advisory Committee on Medical Research. "Report of the Pan American Sanitary Bureau Advisory Group on Research in Chagas Disease." Report presented at the first meeting, Washington, D.C., June 18–22, 1962.

Parsons, Dennis J. "Climate and Economic Development." Restricted circulation memorandum of the South Asia Regional Department, World Bank, May 1973.

Perlman, Mark. "Some Economic Aspects of Public Health Programs in Underdeveloped Areas." In *The Economics of Health and Medical Care,* pp. 286–99. Ann Arbor: University of Michigan, 1964.

Perreau, Pierre. *Maladies Tropicales du Bétail.* Paris: Presses Universitaires de France, 1973.

Phillips, John F. V. *The Development of Agriculture and Forestry in the Tropics: Patterns, Problems, and Promise.* New York: Praeger, 1961.

President's Science Advisory Committee. *The World Food Problem.* Report of the Panel on the World Food Supply. 3 vols. Washington, D.C.: Government Printing Office, 1967.

Reddaway, W. B. "The Economics of Under-developed Countries." *Economic Journal* 73 (March 1963):1–12.

Reid, Escott. *Strengthening the World Bank.* Chicago: Adlai Stevenson Institute of International Affairs, 1973.

Reston, Sally. "Mao's Poem Urges Drive on Virulent Snail Fever." *New York Times* (July 30, 1971):7.

Robinson, Edward A. G., ed. *Economic Development for Africa South of the Sahara.* New York: St. Martin's, 1964.

Rodenwaldt, Ernst, ed. *Welt-Seuchen-Atlas: World Atlas of Epidemic Diseases.* 3 vols. Hamburg: Falk-Verlag, 1952–1961.

Rozeboom, Lloyd E. "DDT: The Life-Saving Poison." *The Johns Hopkins Magazine* 22 (Spring 1971):28–32.

Schwerdtfeger, W., ed. *Climates of Central & South America.* World Survey of Climatology, edited by Helmut E. Landsberg, vol. 12. Amsterdam, New York: Elsevier, 1969.

Sharpston, Michael J. "Health and Development." [Review of *Doctor Migration and World Health,* and *Auxiliaries in Health Care.*] *The Journal of Development Studies* 9 (April 1973): 455–60.

Simmons, James Stevens; Tom F. Whayne; Gaylord West Anderson; Harold Maclachlan Horack; and others. *Global Epidemiology: A Geography of Disease and Sanitation.* 3 vols. Philadelphia: Lippincott, 1944–1954.

Southworth, Herman M., and Bruce F. Johnston, eds. *Agricultural Development and Economic Growth.* Ithaca: Cornell University Press, 1967.

Stevens, Carl M. "Health, Employment and Income Distribution." World Employment Programme Research Working Paper. Provisional draft (WEP2–25/WP21). Geneva: International Labour Organisation, August 1975.

Streeten, Paul. "How Poor Are the Poor Countries." In *Development in a Divided World,* edited by Dudley Seers and Leonard Joy, pp. 67–83. Harmondsworth, Eng.: Penguin, 1971.

Thomas, John D. "Some Preliminary Observations on the Ecology of a Small Man-made Lake in Tropical Africa." In *Ecology and Economic Development in Tropical Africa,* edited by David Brokensha, pp. 113–46. Research Series no. 9. Berkeley: University of California, Institute of International Studies, 1965.

Trewartha, Glenn T. *The Earth's Problem Climates.* Madison: University of Wisconsin Press, 1961.

United Nations, Department of Economic and Social Affairs. *Report on the World Social Situation with Special Reference to the Problem of Balanced Social and Economic Development* (E/CN.5/512/rev.1/ST/ESA/24), New York, 1961.

United Nations, Economic and Social Council, Advisory Committee on the Application of Science and Technology to Development. *World Plan of Action for the Application of Science and Technology to Development.* Rev. ed. (E/4962/rev.1/ST/ECA/146), New York, 1971.

United Nations, Economic and Social Council, Committee for Development Planning. "The International Development Strategy: First Overall Review and Appraisal of Issues and Policies." Preliminary report (E/AC.54/L.60). New York, April 1973.

U.S. Agency for International Development, Office of Science and Technology. *The Application of Geochemical, Botanical, Geophysical, and Remote Sensing Mineral Prospecting Techniques to Tropical Areas: State of the Art and Research Priorities.* (Report TA/OST 72-13). Washington, D.C., 1972.

U.S. National Emergency Council. *Report on Economic Conditions of the South.* Washington, D.C.: Government Printing Office, 1938.

Wade, Abdoulaye. *Economie de l'Ouest Africain (Zone Franc): Unité et Crossance.* Paris: Présence Africaine, 1964.

Warford, Jeremy J. "The Role of Economics in Municipal Water Supply: Theory and Practice." Memorandum of the Public Utilities Department, World Bank. Washington, D.C., December 1971.

Webster, Cyril C., and Peter N. Wilson. *Agriculture in the Tropics.* London: Longman, 1966.

Weisbrod, Burton A. *Economics of Public Health: Measuring the Economic Impact of Diseases.* Philadelphia: University of Pennsylvania Press, 1961.

————, and others. *Disease and Economic Development: The Impact of Parasitic Diseases in St. Lucia.* Madison: University of Wisconsin Press, 1973.

Winslow, Charles E. A. *The Cost of Sickness and the Price of Health.* WHO Monograph Series no. 7. Geneva: World Health Organization, 1951.

World Bank. "Background Paper on Health." Restricted circulation memorandum of the Development Economics Department, October 1974.

————. "The Non Fuel Mineral Industry." Restricted circulation sector working paper of the Industrial Projects Department: Washington, D.C., November 1973.

————. *Health: Sector Policy Paper.* Washington, D.C., March 1975.

————. "World Bank Lending for Livestock Development in Latin America." Restricted circulation memorandum of the Agriculture Projects Department, October 1971.

World Health Organization. *Expert Committee on Trypanosomiasis: First Report.* WHO Technical Report Series no. 247. Geneva, 1962.

————. "Fourth Report on the World Health Situation, 1965–1968." *Official Records of the World Health Organization.* No. 192. Geneva, June 1971.

————. *Onchocerciasis: Its Public Health Importance and Prospect of Control.* Geneva, March 1967.

————. *Schistosomiasis Control: Report of a WHO Expert Committee.* WHO Technical Report Series no. 515. Geneva, 1973.

————. "Selected Helminthic Infections—Results of Surveys, 1963–1968." *World Health Statistics Report* 22 (1969):510–25.

————. *Snail Control in the Prevention of Bilharziasis.* WHO Monograph Series no. 50. Geneva, 1965.

————. *WHO Expert Committee on Malaria, Sixteenth Report.* WHO Technical Report Series no. 549. Geneva, 1974.

Wright, A. C. S., and J. Bennema. *The Soil Resources of Latin America.* FAO/Unesco Project, World Soil Resources Reports no. 18. Rome: Food and Agriculture Organization of the United Nations, 1965.

Wrigley, Gordon. *Tropical Agriculture: The Development of Production.* New York: Praeger, 1969.

Yudelman, Montague. "Imperialism and the Transfer of Agricultural Techniques." Restricted circulation memorandum of the Agriculture and Rural Development Department, World Bank. Washington, D.C., August 1972.

Index

oriental sore [leishmaniasis], 78
Overseas Food Corporation, 18

P

Pacific islands, 13
Paddock, Elizabeth
  quoted, 10n, 32, 33
Paddock, William
  quoted, 10n, 32, 33
Pakistan, 34, 35
Panama, 17
Panama Canal, 67, 78, 79, 83
Pan American Health Organization, 85
Papua New Guinea, 13
parasites
  in animals, 31, 38–42
  in humans, 59–60, 63, 65, 74, 75–76
Parsons, Dennis J., 29n, 46n
peas, 50
Perlman, Mark, 18n
Peru, 47, 49, 59
pesticide, 35–36, 41, 52, 65, 68, 69, 74, 88
Philippines, 16, 18, 25, 27, 28, 49
pigeonpeas, 50
pinworms, 75
plinthite, 25n
poor countries, see also Tropics
  defined, 4
  mineral exploitation in, 53
  soil exploitation in, 22
population
  distribution and disease, 12n, 20, 39, 67, 71–74, 87, 89
  growth and disease, 68
  projects, 87
potatoes, 47, 49
poultry, 18
President's Science Advisory Committee [United States]
  report quoted, 30–31, 43, 46–47

Pritchard, William R.
  quoted, 31
projects, 18, 52, 63, 83, 86, 87–88
protein
  and malnutrition, 29
  in soil, 28–29
  and trypanosomiasis, 39
protozoa, 23, 39

Q

Queensland, 18, 44

R

rainfall, 15–17, 24
Reddaway, W. B.
  quoted, 8
research
  crop, 44–47, 49, 50, 51
  health, 82–83
  investment for, 11, 51–52, 82, 90
  livestock, 43–44, 51
  priorities, 47–48, 89
Reston, Sally, 62n, 77n
Reynolds, G. W., 58n
Rhodesia, 25, 35, 68
rice, 16, 18, 32, 45, 46, 47, 49, 50, 51, 52
Richard Toll scheme, 18
rich countries
  defined, 4
  geographical distribution of, 6–7
river blindness, 59, 69, 71–75, 89
  effects, 69, 71, 74
  etiology, 74
  geographical distribution of, 69, 72–73
  treatment, 74–75

The most recent editions of Catalog of Publications, describing the full range of World Bank publications, and World Bank Research Program, describing each of the continuing research programs of the Bank, are available without charge from:

The World Bank
Publications Unit
1818 H Street, N.W.
Washington, D.C. 20433
U.S.A.

BCL - 3rd ed.